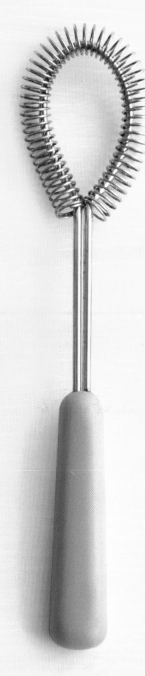

Sign up to my free newsletter at *www.annabelkarmel.com* for exclusive recipes and expert advice

hello.

Welcome to my brand new spring magazine! Discover fresh and delicious recipes for all your family, now the sunshine is here.

After a long, dark winter, it's a wonderful relief to wake up to spring. It's the perfect time to try fresh new flavours, use colourful fruit and vegetables and bring bright zingy tastes to your family's meals.

There's plenty to celebrate this spring. Try my best ever pancake recipe with lots of lovely filling options, enjoy the Easter break with a special seasonal family lunch, and get your children to work on cute and tasty Easter goodies. They'll love making them, and enjoy eating them even more! A spring party is a wonderful excuse for lots of yummy and colourful food – check out my party chapter for some show-stopping spring party treats.

A sunny spring day is the perfect occasion for the first picnic of the year – have a look at my picnic and lunchbox ideas for lots of delicious outdoor inspiration.

Dr Adam Fox has some really valuable advice about helping with eczema, and I've gathered together my best tips for helping a fussy child enjoy good food!

Annabel Karmel

Meet Annabel at Haven...

annabel karmel

Haven Holidays have **36 fabulous** fun-packed family Holiday Parks all around the UK, and with so much choice there's sure to be a Park within just a short drive - perfect for a break with your little ones! Plus, with **2008 prices held** for 2009, there's no better time to book your family holiday.

...and this year, **there's even more on offer** with our exclusive **Annabel Karmel breaks!**

NEW FOR 2009 on all Parks!
Annabel's Creative Kitchen

"Getting children interested in what they eat is the first step to getting them to try new things" says Annabel Karmel MBE, our favourite baby and child food expert and UK's leading author on family nutrition.

Let our FunStars help your kids' creativity run wild with these brand new hands on, up front and messy cookie and cake decorating sessions. It's lots of fun and lots of mess... but here's the good bit, we do the cleaning up!

Have fun all year round with Annabel's Creative Kitchen. And for even more fun, why not come along at Easter, Summer or Halloween for some extra special cakes and cookies for the children to prepare in our Creative Kitchen sessions?

Lots and lots for tiny tots...
- ✔ Little Cubs Club for 1-4 year olds
- ✔ Learn2Swim
- ✔ Fun Activities - with musical instruments, Making Day, Explorer Day
- ✔ Family Fun Shows - Pantomimes, FunStars, Meet the Zoo Troop

...And Mums & Dads too
- ✔ Luxury Spa's ✔ 9-Hole Golf Courses
- ✔ Fishing & Boating Lakes ✔ Pilates
- ✔ Cabaret, Bars & Shows ✔ NEW Mash & Barrel

4 night breaks from only £99* for the whole family

Plus so much more to make it easier for you...
- ✔ Kids' Alive Healthy Eating menu
- ✔ Highchairs & cots for hire
- ✔ Family friendly restaurants with bottle warming facilities, bibs & wipes and childrens' menus
- ✔ Home from home fully equipped Self-Catering Holiday Homes

4 night midweek breaks just got even better - here's your chance to meet Annabel in person!

Monday 20 April - Hafan y Môr, North Wales

Monday 4 May - Devon Cliffs, Devon

Monday 22 June - Combe Haven, East Sussex

Monday 14 September - Haggerston Castle, Northumberland

LITTLE CUBS   ZOO TROOP   LEARN2SWIM

98

Annabel Karmel
annabel karmel **Family Cookbook**

contents

recipes

Family Favourites

Spring Picnic

Happy Easter

Annabel Karmel
Family Cookbook

ART & DESIGN

ART EDITOR Sarah Bridges

PHOTOGRAPHY Dave King

FOOD STYLIST Seiko Hatfield

PROPS STYLIST Jo Harris

MAKE-UP STYLIST Liz Thomas, Jo Penford

REPRO Linda Duong

EDITORIAL

SUB EDITORS Jen Ogilvie, Rachel Zamorski

THANKS TO Rose Catt, Caroline Stearns, Lucinda Kaizik,
Dr Adam Fox, The National Eczema Society

ADVERTISING

ADVERTISING DIRECTOR Sophie Kochan 020 7907 6741

MARKETING Samantha Gould

MANAGEMENT

BOOKAZINE MANAGER Dharmesh Mistry
(020 7907 6100 dharmesh_mistry@dennis.co.uk)

OPERATIONS DIRECTOR Robin Ryan

GROUP ADVERTISING DIRECTOR Julian Lloyd-Evans

CIRCULATION DIRECTOR Martin Belson

FINANCE DIRECTOR Brett Reynolds

GROUP FINANCE DIRECTOR Ian Leggett

CHIEF EXECUTIVE James Tye

CHAIRMAN Felix Dennis

A DENNIS PUBLICATION

Dennis Publishing, 30 Cleveland St, London W1T 4JD.
Company registered in England.
Text © Annabel Karmel & Dennis Publishing Limited; photography
© Dave King, DK & Ebury Press. Licensed by Felden 2009, and may
not be reproduced in whole or part without the consent
of the publishers.
Dennis Publishing operates an efficient commercial reprints
service. For more details please call 020 7907 6100

LIABILITY

While every care was taken during the production of this
bookazine, the publishers cannot be held responsible for the
accuracy of the information or any consequence arising from it.
Dennis Publishing takes no responsibility for the companies
advertising in this bookazine.

Printed at BGP, Bicester

The paper used within this bookazine is produced from sustainable
fibre, manufactured by mills with a valid chain of custody.

112   155

Fresh tastes for your baby

Wake up your baby's tastebuds with these tasty fresh food ideas, and enjoy a wonderful first spring together. These special recipes use natural ingredients to make delicious, nutritious and seasonal meals for your baby.

Fresh tastes for your baby

For spring, I've chosen tasty dishes that will introduce your baby to special versions of meals that we all enjoy. These are special baby-friendly recipes – every ingredient is safe for your baby, and the meals are nutritionally balanced and satisfying for a tiny tummy.

Orchard Fruits with Blueberry

Porridge with Apple, Pear and Apricot

PHOSPHATES AND CHIPS?

Phosphates have a direct impact on aquatic life. Our effective dishwasher tablets are based on phosphate-free plant and mineral ingredients, so there'll be plenty more fish in the sea for your kids to enjoy (and their kids, and their kids, and...).

IT'S ECOLOGICAL

ECOLOGICAL
DISHWASHER
TABLETS
DUAL ACTION
EFFECTIVE CLEANING AND DEGREASING

25 TABLETS
500g ℮

ECOVER®

for people who care

For exciting competitions and fun games, visit **www.its-ecological.com**

Chicken with Spring Vegetables

chicken with spring vegetables

■ Age: 6 months+ ■ Makes 5 portions ■ Prep time: 6 mins ■ Cook time: 25 mins ■ Suitable for freezing

1 small onion, chopped
½ small sweet red pepper, deseeded and finely chopped
1 clove garlic, crushed
1 tbsp olive oil
1 chicken breast cut into pieces (125g/4½oz)
2 tbsp apple juice
175ml/6fl oz chicken stock
1 medium courgette, chopped (100g/4oz)
200g/7oz sweet potato, peeled and chopped
50g/2oz frozen peas
1 tbsp fresh basil, torn

This includes fresh vegetables as well as good quality protein

Sauté the onion and sweet pepper in the olive oil until softened. Add the garlic and sauté for a further minute. Stir in the chicken and continue to cook for three to four minutes. Pour over the apple juice and stock, then stir in the courgette and sweet potato. Bring to the boil, then cover and simmer for about eight minutes. Stir in the peas and continue to cook for three minutes. Stir in the basil. Chop or purée to the desired consistency.

This **balanced meal** in a single dish is a baby version of a **nutritious** and **tasty** combination that appeals to every age. It will help your baby get used to more **complex** tastes

Provides betacarotene, calcium, protein, vitamin C

This makes a **good introduction to fish** for your baby. **Plaice** is one of the best fish to start with, as it has a **lovely moist, soft texture**

Fillet of Fish with cheesy Vegetable Sauce

- Age: 9 months+ ■ Makes 3 portions
- Prep time: 8 mins ■ Cook time: 15 mins
- Suitable for freezing

1 medium carrot, peeled and sliced (approx 75g/3oz)
40g/1½oz broccoli florets
1 fillet of plaice, skinned (approx 100g/4oz)
Knob of butter

For the sauce
15g/½oz butter
15g/½oz flour
150ml/5fl oz milk
40g/1½oz Cheddar cheese, grated

Steam the carrot for five minutes, add the broccoli and continue to cook for a further seven minutes or until the vegetables are tender. Meanwhile, put the plaice into a suitable microwave dish, dot with butter and microwave on high for approximately 90 seconds. If you don't have a microwave, you could poach the plaice in a small saucepan of milk instead.

To make the cheese sauce, melt the butter, stir in the flour and cook for one minute over a low heat. Gradually whisk in the milk. Bring to the boil, then simmer for a few minutes until thickened and smooth. Remove from the heat and stir in the cheese until melted.

Blend together the steamed vegetables, flaked fish and cheese sauce.

Fillet of Fish with Cheesy Vegetable Sauce

Porridge with Apple, Pear and Apricot

■ Age: 6 months+ ■ Makes 4 portions ■ Prep time: 8 mins ■ Cook time: 8 mins ■ Suitable for freezing

1 apple, peeled, cored and chopped
1 ripe pear, peeled, cored and chopped
4 ready-to-eat dried apricots, chopped
4 tbsp water

For the porridge
150ml/5fl oz milk
15g/½oz porridge oats (3 tbsp)

Put all the fruit into a saucepan together with the water. Cover and cook for about six minutes until tender. Meanwhile, put the milk and porridge oats into a small saucepan. Bring to the boil, then simmer, stirring occasionally, for about three minutes. Combine the fruit and the porridge and blend together.

Dried apricots are one of **nature's great health foods.** Choose ones that haven't been treated with sulphur dioxide, as this can trigger **asthma** and **tummy problems** in susceptible babies

This was very popular with my children when they were babies

Porridge with Apple, Pear and Apricot

Cheese and Peas with Orzo

Peas offer twice the protein of most vegetables

cheese and Peas with Orzo

■ Age: 6 months+ ■ Makes 1 portion ■ Prep time: 5 mins ■ Cook time: 12 to 15 mins ■ Suitable for freezing

2 tbsp orzo
1 tbsp frozen peas
1 tbsp crème fraîche or double cream
20g/¾oz Cheddar cheese, grated
1 tsp Parmesan cheese, grated

Cook the orzo according to the instructions on the packet. Add the peas for the final minute of cooking. Drain well and return to the saucepan over a low heat. Stir in the crème fraîche or cream and bubble for two minutes. Remove from the heat and stir in the Cheddar until melted. Allow to cool slightly before stirring in the Parmesan.

Orzo is small, rice-shaped pasta. It is easy to swallow and good for introducing texture to older babies

Rice mixed with veg is an easy next step after purées

Butternut squash is readily available in supermarkets and is **rich in vitamin A**. If you can't get hold of any, though, don't worry – you can make this **cheerful** risotto with **pumpkin** instead

Risotto with Butternut Squash

Risotto with Butternut Squash

- Age: 9 months+ ■ Makes 4 portions
- Prep time: 8 mins ■ Cook time: 25 mins
- Suitable for freezing

60g/2½oz onion, chopped
25g/1oz butter
100g/4oz basmati rice
150g/5oz butternut squash, chopped and peeled
450ml/15fl oz boiling water
3 ripe tomatoes, skinned, deseeded and chopped
(approx 225g/9oz)
50g/2oz Cheddar cheese, grated

Sauté the onion in half the butter until softened, then stir in the rice until well coated. Pour over the boiling water, cover and cook for eight minutes over a high heat. Stir in the butternut squash, reduce the heat and cook, covered, for 12 minutes or until the water has been absorbed.

Meanwhile, melt the remaining butter in a small pan, add the tomatoes and sauté for two to three minutes. Stir in the cheese until melted. Mix the tomato and cheese mixture with the cooked rice.

Blueberries' amazing colour is key to their fantastic health benefits, as their anthocyanins, or pigments, are powerful antioxidants. They also contain Vitamins C and E, so they're a wonderfully healthy food for your baby, and taste great too

Orchard Fruits with Blueberry

■ Age: 6 months+ ■ Makes 2 to 3 portions ■ Prep time: 3 mins ■ Cook time: 5 mins ■ Suitable for freezing

1 eating apple
1 ripe pear, peeled, cored and chopped
40g/1½oz blueberries
1 tbsp baby rice or ½ crumbled rusk (optional)

Put all the fruit into a heavy-based saucepan. Cover and cook over a low heat for about five minutes. Purée in a blender and stir in the baby rice or crumbled rusk (if using).

Adding baby rice or rusk helps introduce your baby to texture

Orchard Fruits with Blueberry

Feeding your baby

Starting your baby on solid foods might seem scary, but it doesn't need to be – enjoy introducing new tastes and this can be a fantastic time for both of you.

The Myths and Truths of Feeding Your Baby

■ Advice on weaning your baby

Introducing a baby to solid food is one of the most exciting moments of parenthood. Or it should be. Unfortunately, as soon as new parents consult books, websites, friends or even doctors for guidance, excitement turns into anxiety. By the time a new parent has absorbed all the popular myths, feeding a baby seems more like a risky science experiment than the fun and enriching experience it should be.

This undue apprehension and excessive cautiousness has sad consequences for child nutrition. Parents feed their babies a bland and limited diet or, worse still, boring, processed food in jars that are marketed to seem safer than home-cooked food. In the process, babies miss an opportunity to develop their taste buds, at the very age when they're most receptive to new tastes. This is one of the reasons kids turn into fussy eaters and can develop bad eating habits that may last a lifetime.

From food allergies to preparing and cooking baby foods, I can give you the confidence to make informed decisions when it comes to weaning your baby and preparing a variety of nutritious, homemade meals on which your baby will thrive.

■ Solids before six months

The current UK Department of Health guidelines state that babies shouldn't begin weaning until they're six months old and should be exclusively breastfed until this time. While in an ideal world breastfeeding exclusively for six months gives your baby a very good start in life, only a small percentage of mothers in the UK are still breastfeeding up to six months. Most health professionals recognise that many babies show signs that they're ready for weaning at an earlier age (but not before 17 weeks). For example, your baby may no longer be satisfied by his usual milk feed, or wake during the night when previously he slept through, and might not be thriving on breast milk alone if for some reason you're not able to produce enough milk.

> " A low-fat, high-fibre diet is good for adults, but not appropriate for babies "

I believe in following your instincts as a mother. Some babies may need simple solids like root vegetable purées or apple, pear or banana from around five months. However, if there's a history of allergy in the family or atopic illness such as eczema, hayfever or asthma, it's best to try breastfeeding exclusively for six months before introducing solids.

Babies' and toddlers' needs are different from an adult's – a low-fat, high-fibre diet is good for adults but not appropriate for babies or young children, as they need more fat and concentrated sources of calories and nutrients to fuel their rapid growth. They shouldn't be given too much fibre either, as it tends to be bulky

"Root vegetables like sweet potato or carrot make ideal first foods"

and can fill them up before they get all the nutrients they need for proper growth and development.

Excess fibre can remove valuable minerals and cause other problems like diarrhoea. Babies should eat a wide variety of fruit and vegetables to make sure they have plenty of vitamins and minerals in their diet. After the first few weeks of weaning, ensure that as well as fruit and vegetable purées you give foods that are higher in calories, like mashed avocado, fruit mixed with Greek yoghurt or vegetables in a cheese sauce.

■ Why homemade purées?

What's the point in giving bland tasteless food such as baby rice when you can introduce your baby to fresh fruit and vegetables? Root vegetables like sweet potato or carrot make ideal first foods due to their naturally sweet flavour and smooth texture once puréed, plus they're rich in betacarotene. Cooked apple or pear are a gentle first

weaning food with an extremely low likelihood of intolerance, and they contain pectin, which helps little bowels to start processing solids efficiently. They also contain vitamin C to boost your baby's immune system.

There's nothing wrong with relying on the odd jar of commercial baby food. The problem is that their nutritional content is compromised because of the heat treatment necessary to make them safe to eat throughout a long shelf life. The foods also tend to be bland, which can make the eventual transition to family food more difficult.

■ Making your own purées

If you're a busy mum and you don't think you have the time to prepare fresh baby food, think again. Lots of fruits such as banana, peaches and avocado don't require any cooking and can simply be mashed to make instant baby food.

As a baby only eats tiny amounts, especially in the early stages of weaning, it saves time to make up larger quantities of purées and freeze them in ice cube

▲ *It saves time to make up larger quantities of purées and freeze them in ice cube trays.*

trays. If you freeze your purées as soon as they're cool and cover with a lid, they're as nutritious as fresh and will remain so for about eight weeks in the freezer. Also, cooking implements like saucepans and ice cube trays don't need to be sterilised.

You don't need to exclusively use fresh vegetables in baby purées. Frozen vegetables are frozen within hours of being picked, thus locking in vital nutrients. Often they're fresher than fresh veggies. Normally, once a food is frozen, it can't be defrosted and refrozen. However, this doesn't apply to frozen vegetables, so if frozen peas, for example, are cooked in a purée or other recipe they can be refrozen and reheated.

Babies enjoy food that tastes good. Sometimes combining fruit with savoury dishes is a good way to get children to eat new foods, and since we can't add salt to baby food, include garlic, herbs and cheese to give flavour. For most babies, it's fine to introduce a different food each day. However, if there's a history of allergy in the family, wait two or three days to be sure there's no reaction to the food you're offering.

You should try introducing more lumpy food at seven or eight months, as chewing helps develop the muscles your baby needs for speech. Stir tiny pasta shapes into your baby's favourite purées and start mashing or finely chopping instead of blending.

▼ *Combining fruit with savoury dishes is often a good way to get children to eat new foods.*

▲ *The amount of food one baby needs to maintain the same growth rate as another child can be completely different, even if the babies are of the same age and weight.*

■ Vegetarian babies

It's fine to raise your baby on a vegetarian diet. However, an adult vegetarian diet isn't suitable, as it's too bulky and high in fibre. Wholegrain cereals are a good source of iron, but don't give your baby too many or he'll feel full without having the nutrients he needs to grow. The early stages of weaning will be just the same as for any other baby, but after six months include nutrient-dense foods like cheese, and from six or seven months incorporate iron-rich foods like lentils, eggs, spinach and dried apricots. While it's true that formula milk should be your baby's main drink for the first year, it's fine to use full-fat cow's milk on your baby's cereal or when making up recipes like cheese sauce.

■ Avoiding alleged allergens

Unless there's a history of allergy in the family, there's currently no conclusive evidence that early diet restrictions help to prevent allergies. In fact, the weaning diet in many developing and non-Western countries is very high in peanut-containing products from as early as four months and the incidence of peanut allergy in these countries is very low.

For babies with no history of allergy in the family, it's fine to give peanut butter and other finely ground nuts from seven months. However, if there's a history of allergy or your baby suffers from eczema, seek medical advice first.

Similarly, a whole egg is perfectly healthy for babies. Just make sure the yolk and white are cooked until solid – a well-cooked scrambled egg, mini omelette or boiled egg mashed into a cheese sauce with vegetables are fine. Egg allergies are less common than most people think. Mild sensitivity is more common than actual allergy, but the effects (such as hives) are relatively untroubling. Since they may not recur each time your child eats an egg, you don't need to enforce a strict no-egg policy unless the reactions get progressively worse.

It's also important to give oily fish like salmon, as it's one of the richest sources of

"Try introducing more lumpy food at seven or eight months"

essential fatty acids, which are beneficial to brain and visual development. Just watch for a reaction when you offer fish on the first few occasions.

■ How much to give

Most babies are naturally quite chubby, but slim down when they become more active. The amount one baby needs to maintain the same growth rate as another can be very different, even if they're the same age and weight. Babies have different metabolic rates and activity levels, and the foods you give them can vary in calorie count. Also, babies have growth spurts when they need to eat more. If your baby is growing and seems content, feed a meal until he loses interest.

Weaning a baby from milk to solids is an exciting time and a big step for both of you. Your baby is entering a whole new world of taste, and eating is one of the great joys of life. Babies generally roughly double their weight at six months and treble it at one year.

The Annabel Karmel & Lindam weaning range is an innovative and practical set that will help babies progress from first tastes to feeding themselves.

The 10-piece weaning set includes a mess mat, bib, feeding spoon, non-spill cup, small bowl, cutlery case, large bowl with finger food tray, and a spoon and 'foon'. This stylish, stain proof range comes in bright red.

Available from Asda, Tesco, Mothercare, John Lewis, Boots and all good retailers.

▲ *Weaning can be a messy process. Make your child's first mealtimes easy and fun with this durable 10-piece weaning set.*

Sharing sweet and homemade heart-shaped treats with your partner and family on Valentine's Day is a delicious way to remember just how much love makes our world go round.

WIN HEARTS ON VALENTINE'S DAY

Valentine's dinner for two

♥ MENU ♥

Spring Salad
with Blue Cheese and Pecans

~

Mild King Prawn Curry

~

Raspberry and Elderflower Jelly
with Fresh Raspberries

Spring Salad with Blue Cheese and Pecans

SPRING SALAD WITH BLUE CHEESE AND PECANS ♥

■ Prep time: 8 mins   ■ Cook time: 10 mins

1 tbsp sunflower oil
1 medium onion, sliced
Knob of butter
100g/4oz pecan nuts
2 tbsp caster sugar
1 bag mixed salad leaves
150g/5oz blue cheese, chopped into small cubes
2 tbsp balsamic vinegar
Salt and freshly ground black pepper

Heat the oil in a frying pan. Add the onion and slowly sweat until soft, then increase the heat to caramelise it. Tip into a large mixing bowl. Melt the butter in the same pan, then add the pecans and sugar and toast over a high heat until caramelised. Tip into the mixing bowl. Add the salad leaves, blue cheese and balsamic vinegar, then toss together and season with salt and pepper.

MILD KING PRAWN CURRY

Prep time: 8 mins **Cook time: 10 mins**

1 tbsp sunflower oil
1 large onion, finely chopped
2 cloves garlic, crushed
½ green chilli, finely diced
1 red pepper, deseeded and finely diced
1 tbsp garam masala powder
400g/14oz tin chopped tomatoes
260ml/9fl oz water
50g/2oz creamed coconut
1 tbsp tomato purée
1 tbsp mango chutney
450g/1lb raw king prawns
Salt and freshly ground black pepper
About 300g/11oz rice, to serve

Heat the oil in a large saucepan. Fry the onion, garlic, chilli and red pepper for five minutes until almost soft. Stir in the garam masala, then add the tinned tomatoes, water, creamed coconut, tomato purée and mango chutney. Bring to the boil, cover with a lid and simmer for 20 minutes. Add the prawns and keep stirring over the heat until they turn pink and are cooked through. Season with salt and pepper and serve with rice cooked according to the instructions on the packet.

Make this **aromatic curry** a little ahead. Then while it cooks, you're **both** free to enjoy a **well-earned glass of wine**

when serving up, arrange the prawns in a heart shape for your loved one

Mild King Prawn Curry

RASPBERRY AND ELDERFLOWER JELLY

■ Prep time: 10 mins plus 6 hours or overnight in the fridge to set ■ Cook time: 2 mins

7 leaves gelatine (about 12g/½oz powdered gelatine)
200ml/6½fl oz Ocean Spray Cranberry and Raspberry Cordial
400ml/13½fl oz sparkling elderflower drink
200g/7oz fresh raspberries

Soak the gelatine leaves in a small bowl of cold water for five minutes. Squeeze any water from the gelatine and place in a small heatproof bowl over a pan of simmering water until melted. Measure the cordial and elderflower into a jug, then add the gelatine and stir together.

Divide the raspberries between four small cups or champagne flutes. Pour the liquid over the raspberries and transfer to the fridge for a minimum of six hours or overnight if possible to set.

This **simple, fresh-tasting** homemade jelly is a **light** and **refreshing** dessert, perfect for finishing off a special evening meal

Raspberry and Elderflower Jelly

RED VELVET CUPCAKES

■ Serves 12 ■ Prep time: 20 mins ■ Cook time: 23 mins

For the cupcakes
55g/2oz Bournville chocolate
55g/2oz softened butter
65g/2oz dark brown sugar
2 large eggs
4 tbsp soured cream
80g/3oz self raising flour
1 tsp baking powder
Pinch of salt
30g/1oz dried cranberries tossed in a little self raising flour to coat
2 tsp red food colouring

For the frosting
2 vanilla pods
200g/7oz softened butter
250g/8oz cream cheese
400g/14oz sieved icing sugar

Preheat the oven to 200C/400F/Gas Mark 6. Melt the Bournville chocolate in a bowl over a pan of just simmering water until melted. Put the remaining ingredients, except cranberries, into the bowl of an electric mixer and mix together until just combined. Then fold the cranberries into this mixture before adding the melted chocolate. Spoon into 12 muffin cases in a muffin tin. Bake for 20 minutes until risen and firm to the touch. Leave to cool in the tin for a few minutes then transfer to a wire rack to cool completely.

To make the frosting, scrape the vanilla seeds from the pods into a bowl, then add the butter and cream cheese. Beat well, then gradually add the sugar four tablespoons at a time until the icing is smooth. Once the cakes are cool, pipe the icing on top using a large star nozzle. Cakes are suitable for freezing without icing.

These **chocolatey** cupcakes have an incredibly **intense** colour. You can decorate them with little **heart biscuits** for a final **Valentine's** touch

Red Velvet Cupcakes

Why not try decorating the cheesecake with extra strawberries?

Heart-Shaped Strawberry Cheesecake

This **creamy** and **delicious** cheesecake makes a **lovely dessert** on Valentine's Day. The **sweet strawberries** are a welcome hint that **summer is on its way**

HEART-SHAPED STRAWBERRY CHEESECAKE

■ **Serves 4** ■ **Prep time: 20 mins** ■ **Cook time: 5 mins**

For the filling
350g/12oz strawberries, halved
200g/7oz caster sugar
2 tbsp water
5 leaves gelatine
400g/14oz full fat cream cheese
1 tsp vanilla essence

For the biscuit base
100g/4oz digestive biscuits, crushed
50g/2oz butter, melted

Put the strawberries, caster sugar and water into a saucepan. Simmer until the strawberries are soft and the sugar has dissolved. Pass the mixture through a sieve into a bowl and allow to cool a little. Meanwhile, soak the gelatine leaves in cold water for about five minutes. Squeeze any water from the gelatine, then add to the warm strawberry mixture, stirring until dissolved. Leave to cool completely.

To make the base, put the biscuits into a freezer bag and crush with a rolling pin. Mix the crushed biscuits with the melted butter, then press firmly into the bases of four heart-shaped springform tins.

Put the cream cheese and vanilla extract into a mixing bowl. Slowly add the cold strawberry mixture and whisk until smooth, then carefully spoon into the tins. Transfer to the fridge and leave to set for about four hours or as long as possible. Decorate with extra strawberries.

HOMEMADE CHOCOLATE TRUFFLES

■ **Makes 50** ■ **Prep time: 20 mins**

350g/12oz plain chocolate
110g/4oz milk chocolate
175ml/6fl oz double cream
50g/2oz unsalted butter at room temperature
1 vanilla pod
Cocoa powder or icing sugar

Break the chocolate into small pieces and put in a heatproof bowl with the cream and butter. Split the vanilla pod, scrape the seeds into the bowl, then add the pod. Put the bowl over a saucepan of simmering water and melt the chocolate and butter, stirring occasionally until smooth and making sure the bowl doesn't touch the water. Remove the vanilla pod.

Transfer the bowl to the freezer and cool for 10 to 20 minutes, stirring every five minutes until the mixture has thickened. Line a baking tray with parchment baking paper. Spoon out mounds of the mixture using a melon baller or teaspoon, and roll between your hands to form a smooth ball.

Refrigerate the truffles for around two hours until firm, then dust with cocoa powder or icing sugar. Store in the fridge and eat within a week.

Homemade Chocolate Truffles

Raspberry and Chocolate Heart Cake

You just have to **fall in love** with this **heavenly combination** of **chocolate, cream and raspberries**. It's a recipe that commands **slavish devotion** from all who taste it

RASPBERRY AND CHOCOLATE HEART CAKE

■ Serves 8 to 10   ■ Prep time: 25 mins   ■ Cook time: 40 mins   ■ Suitable for freezing without icing

For the cake base
180g/6oz butter, softened
180g/6oz caster sugar
180g/6oz self raising flour
30g/1oz cocoa powder
3 large eggs
2 tbsp milk

For the filling
200ml/6½fl oz double cream
150g/5oz raspberries

For the icing
100g/4oz dark chocolate
30g/1oz unsalted butter
2 tbsp raspberry jam

Pouring cream, to serve

Preheat the oven to 180C/350F/Gas Mark 4. Grease and line the base of a 20cm/8in heart-shaped (or round) sandwich tin. Mix together all of the cake ingredients in a bowl using an electric whisk until smooth. Spoon into the tin and level the top. Bake for 35 to 40 minutes until the cake is well risen and shrinking away from the sides of the tin. Remove from the tin and leave to cool on a wire rack.

To make the filling, whisk the cream until stiff, then fold in the raspberries. Slice the cooled cake in half through the middle and spread the cream mixture over the bottom half. Put the top layer on top of the cream and press down.

For the icing, melt the jam in a saucepan until runny, then spread over the top of the cake. Melt the chocolate and butter together in a small heatproof bowl over a pan of simmering water, making sure the bowl doesn't touch the water, then leave to cool and thicken slightly. Spread over the top of the cake but not down the sides. Leave to set for one hour, then serve with pouring cream if you like.

Sprinkling petals over the cake adds a pretty finishing touch

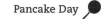

A FLIPPIN' BRILLIANT PANCAKE DAY

Shrove Tuesday was traditionally the day to use up rich food before Lent. Pancakes are a great way to use up whatever ingredients you have to make a fresh and hot meal.

My tried and tested **pancake recipe** works just as well with **savoury** or **sweet fillings**. The trick is to get the pan good and hot before you put the batter in. As for **tossing the pancakes** – give it a go if you dare!

The classic lemon and sugar combo is hard to beat

MY FAVOURITE PANCAKES

■ Makes 12 ■ Prep time: 5 mins
■ Cook time: 20 mins

120g/4½oz plain flour
Generous pinch salt
210ml/7fl oz milk
90ml/3fl oz water
60g/2oz butter

Sift the flour and salt into a large mixing bowl, make a well in the centre and add the eggs. Use a whisk or wooden spoon to incorporate the eggs into the flour. In a separate bowl, mix together the milk and water, then gradually beat this into the egg and flour mixture until the batter is smooth with the consistency of cream. Alternatively, you can simply put all the ingredients into a blender and whiz for a minute.
To make the pancakes, use a heavy-based 18cm (7in) frying pan. Melt the butter and stir two tablespoons of it into the batter. Pour the remaining butter into a bowl. Leave the batter to stand for five minutes.

Using a pastry brush, brush the base of the pan with the melted butter. Get the pan really hot before pouring in the batter, then turn down the heat to medium. If the first pancake sticks, the pan isn't hot enough. You'll need about two tablespoons of batter for each pancake, and it's a good idea to use a ladle so the batter goes into the pan in one go. Tilt the pan quickly until the base is covered with a thin layer of batter.

Cook over a moderate heat for about a minute until you can see the pan through the batter and the edges begin to lift. Slide a palette knife under the pancake and flip it over. Cook the second side for about 30 seconds. The first side of the pancake should have a pretty lacy pattern, while the second side will be spotted with brown.

Brush the pan with melted butter each time before adding the next lot of batter. The best way to do this is to fold up some kitchen paper, dip it in the melted butter and wipe this around the pan to grease it.

Serve the pancakes with the lacy side out and your favourite toppings and fillings.

CHEESE AND HAM CRÊPES

■ Makes 4 ■ Prep time: 15 mins ■ Cook time: 22 mins

15g/½oz butter
15g/½oz plain flour
200ml/7fl oz milk
¼ tsp Dijon mustard (optional)
30g/1oz Gruyère cheese, grated
30g/1oz mature Cheddar, grated
4 tbsp Parmesan, grated
4 pancakes (approx 20cm/8in in diameter)
110g/4oz good-quality ham, cut into strips
Salt and freshly ground back pepper

Swap the ham for bacon if you have some in the fridge to use up

Preheat the oven to 200C/400F/Gas Mark 6. Line a baking tray with parchment baking paper. Melt the butter in a saucepan, remove from the heat and stir in the flour to make a roux. Stir or whisk in the milk, a little at a time, then return the pan to a medium heat and cook, whisking constantly, for approximately four minutes, until the sauce is thick and smooth.

Remove from the heat and stir in the mustard (if using) along with the Gruyère, Cheddar and two tablespoons of Parmesan. The sauce should be quite thick. Season to taste with pepper and a little salt (remember that the ham will be quite salty).

Lay the pancakes on a clean, flat surface and spoon a quarter of the sauce in a line down the centre of each pancake. Scatter the ham over the top, then roll up each pancake to make a fat sausage shape. Carefully transfer the filled crêpes to the prepared baking tray, placing them seam side down.

Scatter the remaining Parmesan over the top and bake for 15 minutes until the crêpes are crisp and brown on the edges and base. Transfer to plates using a fish slice and allow to cool slightly before serving.

CHICKEN AND MUSHROOM PANCAKE PARCELS

■ Makes 4 ■ Prep time: 15 mins ■ Cook time: 25 mins

30g/1oz butter
1 tbsp olive oil
150g/5½oz mushrooms, thinly sliced
1 shallot, finely chopped
1 tsp white wine vinegar
1 tbsp plain flour
150ml/5½fl oz milk
½ tsp Dijon mustard (optional)
2 tbsp crème fraîche
200g/7oz cooked chicken, shredded
4 pancakes
30g/1oz Gruyère cheese, grated
2 tbsp grated Parmesan

I have put the Dijon mustard as optional but I personally think that the sauce needs the extra zip as the chicken and mushrooms tend to be slight flavour "dampeners", being fairly neutral themselves. I used chestnut mushrooms.

Preheat the oven to 200/400F/Gas Mark 6. Line a baking tray with baking paper. Melt half of the butter in a large frying pan and add the oil. Sauté the mushrooms over a high heat for 8 to 10 minutes until cooked through and golden. Season with salt and pepper and set aside.

Melt the remaining butter in a medium saucepan and sauté the shallot for five minutes, until soft. Add the white wine vinegar and cook for two minutes then stir in the flour to make a smooth paste. Remove from the heat and whisk in the milk a little at a time to make a smooth sauce. Return to the heat and bring up to the boil, whisking constantly, so that the sauce thickens. Add the mustard, if using, and crème fraîche and simmer for two minutes. Remove from the heat, add the chicken and mushrooms and season to taste with salt and pepper.

Divide the mixture between the four pancakes, mounding it slightly in the centre. Fold the sides of the pancake inwards then fold the top down and the bottom up to enclose the filling in a rectangular parcel. Put the parcels on the prepared baking tray, seam side down.

Scatter the cheeses over the top of the pancake parcels and bake for 15 minutes, until the cheese is golden and the base of the pancakes are brown and crisp. Carefully transfer to plates using a fish slice.

Cheese and Ham Crêpes

Savoury pancakes make a **delicious quick supper** – all you need is a **simple green salad** to go with them. The fillings can be **very hot** when you take the pancakes **out of the oven**, so warn your child to **be careful**

Chicken and Mushroom Pancake Parcels

To freeze strawberries, first gently wash them and pat them dry

Pancakes with Strawberries and Toffee Sauce

PANCAKES WITH STRAWBERRIES AND TOFFEE SAUCE

■ Makes 8 ■ Prep time: 5 mins ■ Cook time: 16 mins

15g/½oz caster sugar
150g/5oz plain flour
2 eggs
250ml/8½fl oz milk
2 tbsp sunflower oil
125g/4½oz light cream cheese
200g/7oz strawberries, sliced

For the toffee sauce
50g/2oz butter
50g/2oz light brown sugar
150ml/5fl oz double cream
½ tsp vanilla essence

Measure the caster sugar and flour into a bowl. Make a well in the centre. Crack in the eggs, then slowly add the milk and beat until smooth. Heat the oil in a small omelette pan. Pour in a little of the mixture and tilt to coat the pan.

Cook the pancake for two to three minutes, then carefully turn over and cook on the other side. Slide onto a plate while you make the rest.

Place one pancake on a board, spread a tablespoon of cream cheese in the centre and arrange a few slices of strawberries on top. Fold two sides into the centre, then fold in half lengthways so you have a rough square shape. Repeat with the remaining pancakes.

To make the toffee sauce, melt the butter in a small pan. Add the sugar and cream and slowly bring to the boil. Remove from the heat and add the vanilla. Pour a little of the sauce over the pancakes.

Banana and Chocolate Pancakes

BANANA AND CHOCOLATE PANCAKES

The carbs and B vitamins in bananas help to boost energy levels

■ Makes 4 ■ Prep time: 8 mins ■ Cook time: 2 mins

50g/2oz milk chocolate, chopped
50g/2oz dark chocolate, chopped
100ml/3½fl oz double cream
2 tbsp golden syrup
2 medium bananas, peeled and sliced
Vanilla ice cream or whipped cream, to serve

You can use all milk chocolate, but it's more sugary so only use 1 tbsp syrup

Put the chocolate, cream and syrup in a small bowl and melt in the microwave in 15-second bursts, stirring well in between, or over a pan of simmering water, stirring occasionally and making sure the bowl doesn't touch the water.

Arrange sliced banana over half of each pancake. Fold the empty half of the pancake over so the banana is wrapped inside the pancake. Transfer to plates and spoon over the chocolate sauce. Serve with vanilla ice cream or whipped cream.

You can make pancakes in advance and freeze them or store them in the fridge for a couple of days, interleaved with greaseproof paper and covered with clingfilm. To reheat, preheat the oven to 180C/350F/ Gas Mark 4. Stack the pancakes on a heatproof plate and cover with foil. Warm in the oven for about 10 minutes. Alternatively you can reheat them in the microwave.

fresh lunchbox ideas

Refresh your packed lunch repertoire with new ideas, to give your child – and yourself – a fresh and tasty break from the same old sandwiches. An empty lunchbox at the end of the day is a satisfying sight.

fresh lunchbox ideas

Sticking with your child's lunchbox favourites is tempting – at least you know they'll get the energy they need to keep them going through the day. But encouraging them to try new foods makes a balanced diet easier and keeps fussiness at bay.

Chicken Caesar Salad

It's **very easy** to make your own delicious Caesar salad. The **croutons** and **dressing** for this salad can be made the **night before**, so all you need to do in the morning is assemble it

mmm... tasty

chicken caesar Salad

■ Serves 1 ■ Prep time: 7 mins ■ Cook time: 3 mins

1 chicken breast, cooked
1 baby gem lettuce, cut into pieces
1 slice thick white bread, crusts trimmed and cut into small cubes
1 tbsp Parmesan cheese, grated
1 tbsp olive oil

For the dressing
2 tbsp mayonnaise
1 tbsp Parmesan cheese, grated
1 tsp lemon juice
½ small clove garlic, crushed
⅛ tsp Dijon mustard
Few drops Worcestershire sauce
Few drops Tabasco sauce (optional)

This classic dressing makes salad leaves taste great

Heat the olive oil in a small non-stick frying pan and add the cubes of bread. Fry, turning occasionally, until golden brown. Remove with a slotted spoon and drain on paper towels.
In a bowl, combine all the dressing ingredients. Mix together the chicken and lettuce and toss with most of the dressing. Pack the grated Parmesan and the croutons in a separate plastic container for your child to scatter over the salad at lunchtime.

Sticky Chicken Skewers

These skewers look intriguing and are fun to eat

Chicken is a **healthy** and **filling** option for lunch and these **sticky skewers taste lovely**. Take out the skewers before you give this to a younger child

Sticky chicken skewers

■ Serves 4 ■ Prep time: 8 mins and 2 hours marinating
■ Cook time: 8 mins

150g/5½oz skinless, boneless chicken breast, cut into 2cm/¾in cubes
3 tbsp pineapple juice
1 tbsp soft light brown sugar
½ tsp soy sauce
You'll also need four skewers, soaked in warm water for 20 minutes

Mix the pineapple juice, sugar and soy sauce together in a medium bowl. Add the chicken, cover and marinate for two hours or overnight in the refrigerator.

Preheat the grill to high. Thread the chicken onto the skewers, reserving the marinade, and place on a foil-lined grill pan. Grill for three to four minutes each side, watching carefully.

Put the reserved marinade in a small saucepan and bring to the boil. Boil hard for three to four minutes until thick and syrupy. Brush over the cooked chicken, then cool the chicken and refrigerate until needed.

this is yummy!

Adding fruit to a salad makes it really appealing. **Pineapple** goes well with chicken and ham

Pineapple Rice Salad

■ Serves 2 ■ Prep time: 8 mins
■ Cook time: 15 mins

110g/4oz cooked chicken or ham, shredded
2 spring onions, thinly sliced
2 rings tinned pineapple, drained and cut into cubes
½ small red pepper, diced
2 tbsp drained tinned sweetcorn
55g/2oz rice
1 tsp rice wine vinegar
2 tsp sunflower oil
½ tsp honey

Cook the rice according to packet instructions and allow to cool. Mix together the vinegar, oil and honey and season with salt and pepper. Stir this dressing into the rice with the chicken, spring onion, pineapple, pepper and sweetcorn. Refrigerate until needed.

Pineapple Rice Salad

Rice is nice

Everyone seems to love **prawn salad**, and this one has a **zesty lemon dressing** which is perfect for spring. I like to use **soft hot dog buns** for this sandwich, but wholemeal bread is also **delicious**

Make favourite sandwiches novel by using different breads

Spring Prawn Salad Sandwich

■ Serves 1 ■ Prep time: 5 mins

1½ tbsp mayonnaise
½ tsp lemon juice
1 spring onion, finely chopped, or ½ tsp chives, chopped
55g/2oz small cooked prawns
1 hot dog bun, split and buttered
2 little gem lettuce leaves, shredded

Mix the mayonnaise, lemon juice and onion together in a small bowl. Pat the prawns dry with kitchen paper and mix into the mayonnaise. Season to taste with salt and pepper. Put half of the lettuce on the base of the bun and spoon on the prawn filling. Top with the remaining lettuce and sandwich with the top of the bun. Wrap in clingfilm and refrigerate until needed.

Spring Prawn Salad Sandwich

BLT with Maple Roasted Bacon

In Canada, you can get fantastic **maple cured bacon**. It's so yummy it inspired me to make this **maple roasted** bacon. Roast extra when you prepare this, as it keeps in the fridge and is wonderful **crumbled** into salads

This sandwich will certainly keep your child going all day

SIZZLIN' BACON mmmm!

BLT with Maple Roasted Bacon

■ Serves 1 ■ Prep time: 5 mins ■ Cook time: 16 mins

4 rashers streaky bacon, rind removed
½ tbsp maple syrup
2 slices bread, lightly buttered
1 tbsp mayonnaise
2 leaves little gem lettuce, shredded
1 small tomato, sliced

As a variation you could add ½ tsp grain mustard to the mayonnaise

Preheat the oven to 200C/400F/Gas Mark 6. Put a wire cooling rack on a baking tray and sit the bacon on the rack. Roast for 12 to 13 minutes until the bacon is starting to crisp.

Carefully brush both sides of the bacon rashers with the maple syrup and roast for a further two minutes. Brush once more and roast for a final two to three minutes, watching carefully. Remove from the oven and allow to cool slightly. If making for a lunchbox, refrigerate the bacon until thoroughly chilled before making the sandwich.

Spread one of the slices of bread with mayonnaise and scatter over the lettuce. Sit the tomato and bacon on top, then sandwich with the second slice of bread. Cut in half diagonally and serve or wrap for the lunchbox.

Apple, Honey and Raisin Muffins

The **honey** and **apple** make these delicious muffins **light** and **moist**. If you don't have a food processor, **grate the apple finely** and beat it together with the wet ingredients, then **fold in** the dry ingredients

Apple, Honey and Raisin Muffins

■ Makes 8   ■ Prep time: 12 mins
■ Cook time: 20 mins   ■ Suitable for freezing

½ large apple, peeled, cored and grated
55g/2oz raisins
30g/1oz chopped semi-dried apple
85g/3oz self raising flour
½ tsp ground cinnamon
½ tsp ground ginger
¼ tsp salt
55g/2oz butter, room temperature
55g/2oz soft light brown sugar
85g/3oz clear honey
½ tsp vanilla extract
1 egg

Fussy children will like these as they won't notice the apple

Preheat the oven to 180C/350F/Gas Mark 4. Line a muffin tin with eight paper cases. Sift the flour, cinnamon, ginger and salt together and set aside. Put the butter, sugar, honey, egg, vanilla and apple in a food processor and whiz for about one minute until well combined (it will look a little curdled, but don't worry).

Add the flour mixture and pulse twice, then scrape down the sides of the food processor and pulse another two or three times. Add the raisins and pulse twice again to just mix in the raisins without chopping them.

Spoon the batter into the prepared tin, filling the paper cases to about half full. Scatter over the dried apple. Bake for 20 to 22 minutes until risen and firm to the touch. Cool for 10 minutes in the tin, then transfer to a wire rack to cool. Store in an airtight box.

Fruity Flapjacks

 ## Yummy oats

The **oats** in these incredibly **moreish flapjacks** mean a **slow energy-release** for your child, and the dried fruit is full of **fibre**. They will keep children going on **busy days**

Fruity Flapjacks

- Makes 8 bars or 16 squares
- Prep time: 10 mins
- Cook time: 35 mins

200g/7oz rolled oats
30g/1oz raisins
30g/1oz sultanas
30g/1oz dried cranberries
30g/1oz desiccated coconut
85g/3oz butter
5 tbsp golden syrup
110g/4oz soft light brown sugar
¼ tsp salt
½ tsp vanilla extract

Preheat the oven to 150C/300F/Gas Mark 2. Line a 20 x 20cm (8 x 8in) square cake tin with baking paper, making sure the paper comes up the sides of the tin.

Put the butter, syrup, sugar and salt in a saucepan and heat gently, stirring occasionally, until the butter has melted. Remove from the heat, stir in the vanilla and set aside to cool slightly.

Put the oats, dried fruits and coconut in a bowl, add the melted mixture and stir well. Press into the prepared tin (a potato masher is good for this) and bake for 35 to 40 minutes until golden brown around the edges.

Remove from the oven and cool for 10 minutes, then mark into bars or squares with a sharp knife. Cool completely in the tin before lifting out and cutting into bars or squares. Store in an airtight container.

World Foods

New recipes from around the world for children from 4 years on, from Annabel Karmel the creator of the successful Eat Fussy range.

We tested recipes with children all over the country and they chose their favourites.

Contributing to your five a day

Available from the chilled aisle in Sainsbury's, Tesco and Ocado.com

new in store

"I think it is very important to introduce children to a wide variety of tastes and flavours early on. But with our busy & hectic lifestyles, this is often difficult. I have created a range of delicious meals based on favourite recipes from around the world. Tried & tested and loved by children, they taste so delicious; you'll want to eat them yourself! Do visit my website www.annabelkarmel.com for homemade recipes & helpful advice."

Annabel Karmel

For kids from 12 months on

NO 1 KIDS meal

Available from Sainsbury's, Tesco, the Co-op, Ocado.com, Budgens & Center Parcs

Tasty prepared meals for hungry kids and busy mums

Wholesome ingredients. No preservatives. No artificial colours. No additives. GM Free. Visit the chilled aisle.

www.annabelkarmel.com

Eczema and Food Allergy

WORDS *Dr Adam Fox*

One in five children suffer from eczema in their early years. What can be done to treat it, and how is it connected to food allergies?

Dr Adam Fox – Consultant Paediatric Allergist
www.adamfox.co.uk

Eczema and food allergy – *the facts*

Many parents make changes to their child's diet to try to improve their skin, but how effective is this?

■ What is eczema?

The past 40 years have seen a dramatic rise in allergic diseases, particularly in the Western world. As well as huge increases in the amount of childhood asthma and hayfever, it's now estimated that atopic or allergic eczema affects almost 20% of children.

Atopic eczema (also known as atopic dermatitis) is a chronic itchy skin condition that most commonly develops in early childhood. Eczema tends to be a variable disease with children suffering from dry skin, which flares up with sore patches from time to time, often for no apparent reason.

Fortunately, for most children, eczema is a relatively mild, albeit still irritating condition. However, for a smaller proportion of children, eczema can be more severe and continuous, having a significant impact on a child's quality of life as well as that of their parents. In a recent survey of parents of children with eczema by the National Eczema Society, one in six mums said they would consider having no more children if those children were also to suffer from eczema.

▲ *In toddlers eczema affects the creases of arms and legs.*

▶ *In infancy, eczema tends to affect the face and limbs.*

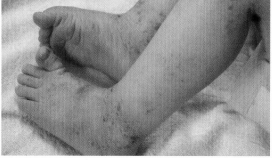

"It is estimated that atopic or allergic eczema now affects 20% of children"

▣ What is the best way to treat eczema?

Conventional medical treatment of eczema revolves around two principles. Emollients (moisturisers) are used regularly all over, together with bath oils, to improve the hydration of the skin. However, these don't prevent the sore, inflamed areas from developing, nor do they calm them down. For these sore or active areas of eczema, anti-inflammatories such as steroid skin creams are needed. And if a bacterial infection has caused the flare-up of eczema, antibiotics must be used too. Parents are often very nervous of using steroid creams because of their possible side effects. When used carefully, under the direction of a doctor, steroid creams are both effective and very safe. However, long-term use can cause skin thinning, which is a particular issue in areas where the skin is already thin such as on the face. Consequently, parental concern over steroids often results in eczema being

requires considerable expertise, and parents should raise their concerns with their family doctor or paediatrician rather than experimenting themselves.

▣ Where there's eczema, there are often food allergies

There appears to have been a large increase in food allergies over recent decades, although this has been less well documented than the rise in other allergic diseases. Peanut allergy, for example, has tripled in just over a decade and now affects almost one in 50 children in the English-speaking world. Food allergies can be broadly divided into immediate allergies, which lead to immediate symptoms such as hives, wheeziness and, in severe cases, anaphylaxis (a life-threatening allergic reaction),

and those that cause more delayed symptoms. Immediate reactions are usually quite obvious when they occur, as they produce symptoms very soon after the food is eaten and can also be confirmed with special allergy tests. Delayed reactions involve a different part of the immune system and may be tricky to diagnose, as symptoms can occur many hours after the food has been eaten and as yet there are no reliable tests to confirm which food is the problem. Eczema may be associated with immediate food allergies, delayed food allergies or both. ▶

"Immediate reactions are usually quite obvious when they occur"

undertreated, which can lead to skin damage.

Eczema can flare up for a variety of reasons, including skin infections, irritants (such as abrasive clothing or sweating) and viral infections. Many parents also worry that their child's diet may be a cause. In fact, studies have shown that 75% of parents have changed their child's diet to try to improve their eczema. Many doctors are sceptical that there's any value in such dietary manipulation, as it may place the child at risk of missing out on essential nutrients and force them to endure the considerable hardship the careful avoidance of any specific food leads to. However, our understanding of the possible role of food allergies in eczema has now improved considerably, and it's becoming increasingly clear that, in some children, identifying and excluding problem foods can have a significant impact on eczema. Identifying the correct foods in the correct children still

▶ *Wheat products, such as bread, are a possible cause of food allergies.*

"Children with severe eczema before six months of age are at risk of developing a food allergy"

▣ Eczema and immediate food allergies

There is a close relationship between eczema and immediate food allergies. Almost all the children in my clinic who have immediate food allergies either have eczema or had it during the first year of life. This strongly suggests that eczema may have a causative role in food allergies, and this is currently the subject of a lot of interest in the scientific world. There is also a clear relationship between the age at which the eczema first appeared, how severe it is and the likelihood of developing food allergies. Studies have shown that children with severe eczema that started before six months of age are at particular risk (and most will have a food allergy), while those who didn't develop eczema until they were over one year old are much less likely to have a food allergy.

Most immediate food allergies are caused by a relatively small number of foods – milk, egg, peanut, tree nuts, fish, shellfish, soy and wheat – although allergies to sesame, kiwi and banana seem to be getting more common. Once an immediate food allergy is diagnosed, there's currently no real alternative to avoiding the food, while also being prepared to treat allergic reactions quickly when they occur. Fortunately,

▶ *Allergies to milk and eggs are often outgrown during the course of childhood.*

many food allergies are outgrown during the course of childhood, particularly those to milk and egg.

▣ Eczema and delayed food allergies

The link between delayed food allergies and eczema remains quite controversial. The suggestion that a child could be regularly eating something that's worsening their eczema still isn't taken seriously by some doctors. While most children with eczema won't be suffering from delayed food allergies, correctly identifying problem foods in the right children can lead to significant improvements in eczema and thus reduce the reliance on steroid creams to keep the skin under control. Research in this area has suggested that milk, egg, soya and wheat are the most likely culprits, and again it's those children whose eczema started early in infancy and is severe who

are most likely to respond to dietary changes. However, the allergy tests used to diagnose immediate allergies, such as skin prick tests or a blood test known as Specific IgE, are of much less value in delayed allergies. Many companies offer food testing over the internet to identify foods that may worsen eczema, but there's no research to support these and they often lead to completely pointless food exclusions. Also, such tests aren't used by allergists or dermatologists. While these tests appear to offer a quick and easy solution, there's currently no substitute for evaluation by an experienced doctor or dietician. After taking a detailed history, they may advise the complete elimination of specific foods and carefully evaluate the results. Even if excluding a particular food does appear to help, it's essential that an attempt to reintroduce the food is made (which would be expected to lead to a worsening of the eczema) to confirm the food is a problem.

Common causes of immediate allergies

- ▣ Milk
- ▣ Egg
- ▣ Peanut
- ▣ Tree Nut
- ▣ Fish
- ▣ Shellfish
- ▣ Soya
- ▣ Wheat

Common causes of delayed allergies

- ▣ Milk
- ▣ Egg
- ▣ Soya
- ▣ Wheat

Should I try excluding foods I suspect to be a problem?

When evaluating a child with eczema, your doctor will pick up on certain clues that raise the possibility of food being a problem. As mentioned earlier, it's children with moderate to severe eczema that starts before six months of age who are most likely to have a food allergy. Certain foods such as tomatoes or citrus fruits can act as an irritant on eczematous skin. This may cause redness and itching, but isn't an allergy and can be avoided by simply rubbing a barrier cream around the mouth before eating.

It's important to remember that food allergy and diet often play no role in eczema and, while it's important to keep an open mind, it's never a good idea to restrict a child's diet without good reason. If removing a food from the diet doesn't seem to help and reintroducing it doesn't make things worse, it's very unlikely to be a problem and shouldn't be further restricted.

What to do if you suspect food is a problem

If you suspect your child has an immediate food allergy or something they're eating is making their eczema worse, you should discuss this with your doctor. They may wish to trial a food exclusion or recommend that your child has some allergy tests. Most large hospitals have a paediatric or dermatology department where one of the doctors has an interest in allergies, and a few large teaching hospitals have specialist paediatric allergists.

Fortunately, most children grow out of their eczema by later childhood and many common food allergies such as milk and egg are also often outgrown. It's therefore important that if a diagnosis of food allergy is made, your child should still receive ongoing follow-up care to check for the possibility that the food could be safely reintroduced. ✿

Never restrict a child's diet without good reason – it may place them at risk of missing out on essential nutrients.

Clues that eczema may be related to diet

- Eczema that first appeared at less than six months of age
- Family history of allergies, such as asthma, eczema, hayfever
- Eczema doesn't respond as well as expected to treatment, such as with steroid creams
- Gastrointestinal symptoms such as colic, reflux, diarrhoea or poor weight gain
- Worsening of eczema after meals including breast milk (think about what you had eaten earlier and consider keeping a food diary to pick up any consistent patterns)
- Presence of one food allergy – if your child has an obvious allergy to one food, consider if another is also causing problems

"If you suspect your child has a food allergy, speak to your doctor"

Waking up the Senses

Excite all your child's senses this spring with fresh food that looks special, smells wonderful, feels good to touch, sounds crunchy – and tastes delicious.

Mini Pea and Prawn Pies

Waking up the Senses

It's easy to get stuck in a rut and serve up the same meals each week, but if you want your child not to grow into a fussy eater it's important to introduce variety into their diet. Now is a great time to awaken their senses with fresh tastes and new dishes.

Spaghetti Carbonara

Feed Your Imagination

Award winning science kits from  interplay

BATH BOMB
Have Fab Fizzy Fun with...
- **Explore**
  - Exciting Effervescent Experiments
  - Fascinating Fizzy Activities

Make colourful bombs and com... loads of fascina... fizzy experime...

Fun & Easy To Do!

www.treetoys.com

PERFUME LABORATORY
Make perfect scents with...
- Fascinating Fragrances
- Absorbing Aroma Activities

...ke your own Heavenly ...mas, Crystal Gel Pourri, ...blime Slime and much, much more!

LUXURY SOAP SCIENCE
Have good clean fun with...
- **Explore**
  - Super Soapy Science
  - Designer Soap Activities

Make wonderful soap creations, blend colours and scents to make designer soaps.

Fun and Easy to do

www.treetoys.com

WILD! science ™

Solar Rainbow Maker
TECHNOKIT
Fill your room with rainbows every time the sun shines!

www.interplayuk.com

Solar Butterfly
Paint the wings!
TECHNOKIT
Stick on to a sunny window, and watch it come to life!
Easy to assemble!

interplay

TECHNOKIT

interplay

Available from all good Toy and Gift stores or online from www.interplaydirect.co.uk

NUMBER ONE 1 FOR SCIENCE & NATURE

Interplay has received 20 awards in the past 9 years
including 3 times winner of 'Good Toy Guide' Best Science and Nature Toy

The warmly aromatic sauce combined
with soft and tasty meatballs makes this
a good dish for introducing herbs and
spices in a child-friendly way

Meatballs and Sweet Potato Tagine

■ Serves 4   ■ Prep time: 30 mins
■ Cook time: 30 mins   ■ Suitable for home freezing

For the meatballs
225g/8oz lean minced beef
150g/5oz red onion, chopped
½ tbsp olive oil
½ clove garlic, crushed
30g/1oz breadcrumbs
½ tbsp chopped parsley
3 tbsp grated Parmesan cheese
Large pinch of black pepper
1 tsp soy sauce
½ tsp soft light brown sugar
2 to 3 tbsp sunflower oil

For the tagine sauce
50g/2oz red onion, chopped
80g/3oz sweet potato, grated
80g/3oz carrot, grated
½ tsp grated fresh ginger
⅛ tsp ground cumin
⅛ tsp ground coriander
⅛ tsp ground cinnamon
Pinch turmeric
400g/14oz tin chopped tomatoes
1 tbsp tomato purée
1½ tsp sun-dried tomato purée
1½ tsp honey
250ml/8½fl oz vegetable stock
(I use a Telma stock cube)
1 tsp fresh coriander leaf, chopped
Salt and freshly ground black pepper

To make the kofta meatballs, sauté the onion in the olive oil for six to eight minutes until soft. Add the garlic and cook for a further minute. Transfer the mixture to a food processor with the remaining ingredients and pulse 8 to 10 times until everything is chopped and combined. Take one-teaspoon measures of the mixture and shape into meatballs.

To make the sauce, sauté the onion, sweet potato and carrot in the oil for 8 to 10 minutes until soft. Add the garlic, ginger and spices and cook for a further minute. Pour in the tinned tomatoes, tomato purées, honey and stock, then bring to the boil. Add the coriander leaf and simmer for 15 minutes.

Meanwhile, dust the koftas with flour and brown in the sunflower oil. Add to the sauce and simmer for five minutes.

This makes a delicious meal for the whole family

Meatballs and Sweet Potato Tagine

Lemon Chicken

The light batter and zesty fresh lemon
make this favourite chicken recipe
really tasty and a pleasure to eat

Lemon Chicken

■ Serves 4 ■ Prep time: 20 mins, plus marinating ■ Cook time: 15 mins

For the chicken
2 large chicken breast fillets, cut into bite-sized chunks
1 tsp soy sauce
1 egg yolk
1½ tbsp cornflour
2 to 3 tbsp sunflower oil, for frying
4 thinly sliced spring onions, to serve

For the sauce
Zest and juice (4 tbsp) 1 large lemon
2 tbsp caster sugar
4 tbsp water
1 tsp cornflour
Salt and freshly ground black pepper

Put the chicken in a bowl and toss with the soy sauce. Leave to marinate for 30 minutes. Whisk together the lemon zest and juice with the sugar, water and cornflour in a small saucepan. Bring to the boil, whisking constantly until thickened, then keep warm.

Meanwhile, heat the oil in a large heavy-based saucepan. Whisk together the egg yolk and cornflour in a small bowl to form a batter. Toss the chicken in the batter and fry for three to four minutes on each side until golden and cooked through.

Transfer to a plate and spoon over the warm lemon sauce. Scatter over the spring onions before serving.

The chicken breast fillets should be about 340g / 12oz

Easy Crispy Duck Pancakes

■ Serves 4 ■ Prep time: 10 mins
■ Cook time: 1½ hours

4 duck legs
½ tsp Chinese five-spice powder
4 tbsp soy sauce
4 tbsp clear honey
½ tsp ginger, grated
12 Chinese pancakes (see opposite)
Plum sauce, to serve
6 spring onions, shredded lengthways
½ small cucumber, cut into matchsticks

Preheat the oven to 220C/450F/Gas Mark 8. Rub the duck with the five-spice powder, then sit it on a rack over a roasting tin. Put about ½cm (¼in) of water in the base of the tin to prevent the duck fat from smoking.

Roast the duck for 30 minutes, then reduce the heat to 180C/350F/Gas Mark 4. Mix together the soy sauce, honey and ginger to form a glaze. Remove the duck from the oven and brush the skin with the glaze. Roast for a further 45 minutes, brushing with the glaze every 15 minutes.

Remove the duck from the oven and increase the heat to 200C/400F/Gas Mark 6. Let the duck rest for five minutes, then remove the skin, cut the meat from the bone and shred it using two forks. Put the meat on a baking tray and drizzle over any of the remaining glaze, then cook for a final 10 minutes.

Meanwhile, steam the pancakes and cut the duck skin into small pieces. Remove the meat from the oven and mix together with the crispy skin. Serve with the pancakes, plum sauce, spring onions and cucumber.

Duck pancakes are always popular with my children in Chinese restaurants. The traditional method for cooking duck takes about three days, but my quicker version is just as delicious

For the Chinese pancakes

- Makes 12 ■ Prep time: 30 mins and resting
- Cook time: 20 mins ■ Suitable for freezing

250g/9oz plain flour, plus extra for rolling
180ml/6fl oz boiling water
1 tbsp toasted sesame oil

Put the flour in a bowl and mix together with the water to form a soft dough. It may look a little dry at first, but keep mixing. Turn the dough on to a lightly floured surface and knead for four to five minutes until smooth. Wrap the dough in clingfilm and leave it to rest at room temperature for 30 minutes.

Roll the dough out on a floured surface to about 3mm thick and cut out circles with a 7cm (2½in) round cutter.

Re-roll the trimmings until you have 12 circles. Brush the tops of the circles with sesame oil, then sandwich together in pairs, oiled sides together.

Preheat a large heavy-bottomed frying pan. Roll out the "sandwiches" on a well-floured surface to about 12cm (6in) in diameter. Cook each pair of pancakes in the dry frying pan for 30 to 60 seconds until a few brown spots appear on the base of the pancakes, then flip over and cook for a further 30 to 60 seconds. Transfer the pancakes to a plate and, when cool enough to handle, peel them apart. You may have to look for the seam around the edges.

Stack the pancakes on a plate and cover with clingfilm. Steam for 10 minutes before serving.

You can freeze the pancakes interleaved with baking paper and wrapped in clingfilm followed by foil. Defrost for one to two hours at room temperature.

Be careful when separating the pancakes as hot steam can be released

Easy Crispy Duck Pancakes

Mini Pea and Prawn Pies

■ Serves 4 ■ Prep time: 40 mins
■ Cook time: 20 mins ■ Suitable for freezing unbaked

For the filling
30g/1oz butter
1 small shallot, finely chopped
2 tsp white wine vinegar
30g/1oz plain flour
300ml/10fl oz milk
4 tbsp crème fraîche
225g/8oz cooked prawns
55g/2oz frozen peas

Personal pies are more appetising than a dollop from a big dish

For the topping
600g/1lb 5oz potatoes, peeled and quartered
15g/½oz butter
6 tbsp milk
White pepper
Grated nutmeg
4 tbsp grated Parmesan cheese (optional)
Salt and freshly ground black pepper

To make the mashed potato topping, boil the potatoes in plenty of salted water for 15 minutes or until the tip of a table knife can be inserted easily. Drain and mash with the butter and milk, then season to taste with salt, white pepper and nutmeg.

Melt the butter in a medium-sized saucepan and sauté the chopped shallot for five to six minutes until soft. Add the white wine vinegar and boil for two minutes, then stir in the flour and cook for a further minute.

Remove the pan from the heat and whisk in the milk, a little at a time, then return to the heat and cook, whisking constantly, until the sauce has thickened and come to a boil. Stir in the crème fraîche, then remove from the heat and add the prawns and peas.

Preheat the oven to 200C/400F/Gas Mark 6. Divide the filling between four large ramekins or cups (250ml/8½fl oz capacity) and carefully spread the mashed potato over the top (it's easier to do this if you have time to chill the filling first). Sprinkle over the Parmesan (if using).

Put the ramekins on a baking tray and bake for 20 minutes until the potato is golden and the filling is hot. If baking from chilled, allow an extra 5 to 10 minutes cooking time.

Assembled but unbaked pies can be frozen for up to one month if well wrapped in clingfilm, but make sure the prawns haven't been frozen previously. Defrost overnight in the fridge and bake as above.

Mini Pea and Prawn Pies

Spaghetti Carbonara

This famous Italian dish is
quick to make, yet always tastes so good.
Spinning and sucking up the spaghetti
is fun and rewarding
for children too

Spaghetti Carbonara

■ Serves 2　■ Prep time: 5 mins　■ Cook time: 15 mins

225g/8oz spaghetti
½ tbsp olive oil
125g/4½oz pancetta, diced
125ml/4fl oz double cream
2 egg yolks
50g/2oz Parmesan cheese, grated
Salt and freshly ground black pepper

Cook the spaghetti in a pan of lightly salted, boiling water until al dente. Meanwhile, heat the olive oil in a frying pan and sauté the pancetta for three to four minutes until browned. In a bowl, whisk together the cream, egg yolks, Parmesan, and salt and pepper.

Once cooked, drain the pasta and return to the saucepan. Immediately stir in the egg and cheese mixture until well combined. Add the pancetta, toss with the sauce and heat through. You can thin the sauce with a little extra cream if necessary. Serve straight away with some freshly grated Parmesan.

This fun, messy pasta dish turns a meal into playtime

Cheesy Garlic Bread

Cheesy Garlic Bread

■ Serves 8　■ Prep time: 10 mins
■ Cook time: 20 mins
■ Suitable for freezing, unbaked

85g/3oz butter, softened
2 cloves garlic, crushed
1 tbsp finely chopped parsley
30g/1oz Cheddar cheese, finely grated
30g/1oz Gruyère cheese, finely grated
2 tbsp Parmesan cheese, grated
1 French stick

Preheat the oven to 200C/400F/Gas Mark 6. Mix together the butter, garlic, parsley and cheeses. Slice the loaf in half lengthways and spread each cut side with the butter mixture, then sandwich it back together. Alternatively, slice as pictured here (so the loaf stays whole) and insert mixture.

Wrap the loaf in foil and bake for 20 minutes. If serving straight away, unwrap it and bake for a further two to three minutes to crisp it up. If taking on a picnic, carefully wrap the loaf in a second layer of foil and a double layer of tea towels to keep it warm for up to one hour.

The aroma of this baking will get your child in the mood for food

This mouth-watering classic is really delicious hot from the oven. And it keeps warm for an hour or so – perfect for sharing round if you're out for a spring picnic

Pasta with Tomato and Mascarpone Sauce

Pasta with Tomato and Mascarpone Sauce

■ Serves 2　■ Prep time: 5 mins　■ Cook time: 30 mins

175g/6oz pasta
250ml/9fl oz smooth passata
2 tbsp Mascarpone cheese
1 tbsp light olive oil
1 small onion, finely chopped
1 clove garlic, crushed
50g/2oz sweet potato, peeled and chopped into
small pieces (peeled weight)
150ml water
½ tsp honey
Salt and freshly ground black pepper

Cook the pasta in a large pan of salted water according to the
packet instructions. To make the sauce, heat the oil in a saucepan.
Add the onion and garlic and fry over a low heat, then add the
sweet potato and mix together. Add the passata, bring up to the
boil, cover with a lid and simmer gently for 20 minutes until the
potatoes have softened and the sauce is thicker. Add the water,
then whiz in a food processor until smooth. Add the Mascarpone.
Return to the saucepan and heat gently. Season to taste, then add
the honey. Drain the pasta and toss with the sauce.

Try scattering a little fresh basil over the top of the pasta

This quick pasta dish means no matter how busy your day's been, your children's meal can be ready in record time, yet still be tasty and homemade

Melted Chocolate Puddings

■ Serves 4   ■ Prep time: 30 mins
■ Cook time: 12 mins

150g/5½oz dark chocolate
110g/4oz butter, plus extra melted butter for greasing
1 whole egg
2 egg yolks, at room temperature
3 tbsp caster sugar
½ tsp vanilla
1 tbsp cornflour
4 white chocolate truffles
Vanilla ice cream, to serve

Preheat the oven to 190C/375F/Gas Mark 5. Generously butter four mini metal pudding basins and line the bases with circles of baking paper.

Break the chocolate into small pieces and put it into a heatproof bowl. Add the butter and put the bowl over a saucepan of warm water, making sure the bottom of the bowl doesn't touch the water. Melt the chocolate and butter, stirring occasionally, until smooth, then set aside to cool slightly.

Put the egg, egg yolks, sugar and vanilla in a large bowl and beat, using an electric mixer on high speed, until very pale and about four times its original volume (ribbon stage). This will take four to six minutes. Sift in the cornflour and trickle over the melted chocolate. Fold the flour and chocolate into the eggs until thoroughly combined.

Spoon 2 tbsp of the chocolate batter into the base of the moulds and sit one truffle in each. Spoon in the remaining batter to cover up the truffles. Put the pudding basins on a baking tray and bake for 10 to 12 minutes until just set on the surface.

Remove the puddings from the oven and let them sit for two minutes. Turn them out onto plates and serve straight away with vanilla ice cream.

These puddings look and smell gorgeous. But as you cut into them they get even better, as white chocolate sauce comes flowing out

Melted Chocolate Puddings

DON't LiKE
VEG

i want
CRiSPS

no peas

Fussy Little Eaters

Most children go through a fussy stage, and it can be difficult to get them to eat a balanced, nutritious diet. A creative approach to cooking will encourage your child to try new foods.

Tempting your fussy eater

While fussy eating rarely results in serious nutritional deficiencies, it can be infuriating if your children refuse to eat anything green, or with a passing resemblance to fruit. Luckily, there are ways to make them more adventurous

Tasty meals for hungry kids & busy Mums

Eat Fussy is a range of delicious chilled prepared meals for children from 12 months on.

Tried and tested and loved by children. Choose from Salmon & Cod Fish Pie, Beef Cottage Pie, Tasty Chicken & Rice and many more.

Available from Sainsburys, Tesco, Ocado.com, the Co-op, Center Parcs & Budgens.

▲ *Never worry that you're on your own! It can be time consuming coming up with ideas to tempt your child, but these tasty prepared meals are specially designed for fussy eaters. Look out for them in your local supermarket.*

■ **You're not alone**

It is hugely frustrating when your child is fussy about food, but don't despair. With tried and tested tips, my special recipe ideas and plenty of patience you can persuade your child to try something deliciously new.

Fussy eating is exasperating, boring and also worrying. But one thing's for sure – you're not alone. Nine out of ten children go through at least one long fussy stage. So in fact a child who is open-minded about food is pretty unusual.

Every child is different of course, but there are some picky preferences that many children share: no lumps in sauce, no green bits, no vegetables, chicken only with breadcrumbs... the list goes on!

My son Nicholas was a terribly fussy eater when he was small. So I started inventing tasty recipes that would tempt him to try something new. Now I've collected together all the advice that personally I've found really works.

Of course there is no magic fix for fussiness, but don't be hard on yourself if your child is fussy. By giving fresh ideas a go and aiming to share home-cooked meals as a family, you're trying your best for your child. And trying your best is all you can do. Your child might just take a little (or a lot of) persuading.

When you want your child to enjoy a healthy balanced diet but they'll only eat plain pasta or chips, it's easy to become concerned about their lack of nutrients. Fussiness can create so much stress for parents. Meanwhile children themselves seem perfectly happy to eat the same thing every day. Take solace from the fact that it's actually pretty unusual for fussiness to result in serious nutritional deficiencies. Children tend to grow out of it, eventually.

Take a look through my top tips for fussy eaters, from smuggling vegetables into favourite dishes to involving children in the preparation of their own food. And try some of my specially selected recipes, which have all been successfully tested on fussy kids. I wish you the very best of luck on your journey through your child's fussy stage. There is light at the end of the tunnel, I promise!

■ Eat as a family

Eat together as a whole family whenever possible, as lots of social chat can take the focus off your child's eating. Avoid using mealtimes to assert your authority. If there is a lecture to give, choose another time.

■ Chill out

If your child refuses to eat anything other than junk food, relax. They'll soon discover there isn't much point making a fuss if you don't react.

■ Give lots of praise

Try and make mealtimes a positive experience. Hide your frustration and praise your child excessively when they eat well or try something new. You may need to ignore some bad behaviour to refocus attention on the good behaviour.

■ Disguise veggies

You can sneak vegetables into wraps, lasagne and quesadillas or hide them under grated cheese on pizzas. You can even blend them into a tomato or Bolognese sauce and serve with pasta. Children like eating with their fingers, so give them corn on the cob or sweet potato wedges.

■ Cook together

It's amazing how being involved in the planning and preparation of a meal can stimulate a child's appetite. Invite their friends over for a cooking party, where they prepare their own supper.

■ Serve fresh food from a young age

Start your baby off on fresh baby food rather than jars of processed food. If they're used to a variety of fresh flavours early on, children are less likely to become fussy eaters when you integrate them into family meals.

■ Think small

Give small portions. It isn't good to overload your child's plate. Also, children generally prefer smaller pieces of food, so give them meals like mini burgers with new potatoes, small broccoli florets and mini carrots. They like eating from small containers, so use ramekins to prepare individual portions of foods like fish pie.

■ Be creative

A gift wrapped in bright paper with a ribbon inspires more enthusiasm than one given in a brown cardboard box, and the same goes for food. You can transform a plain peanut butter sandwich into an irresistible treat by cutting it into a heart or a star. If you're making Chinese-style food, let your child eat it using child-friendly chopsticks joined at the top.

■ Choose full fat

If children are underweight and not eating well, they need as much energy (calories) as possible. Choose full-fat dairy products such as cheese, milkshakes or good-quality ice-cream and avoid using low-fat dairy products.

■ Try new recipes

Don't just stick to favourite meals. Offer a variety of healthy dishes and keep trying new recipes. Offering only the foods you're sure your child will eat can encourage extreme fussiness and lead to a restricted and unbalanced diet.

■ Keep snacks healthy

Avoid empty calorie snacks like crisps or soft drinks and keep a supply of healthy snacks on hand – maybe have a low shelf in the fridge with cut-up fresh fruit and other healthy foods. When children are hungry, they won't wait.

■ Let them help with their lunch

Get children involved in packing their own lunchboxes – that way you'll know what foods are acceptable. There are some foods children may eat at home but won't eat in front of their peers. Also, children won't bother with anything that takes a long time to eat.

■ Make your own 'junk' food

Try making your own healthy junk food using good-quality lean meat for burgers and English muffins for pizza bases. A good way to coat homemade fish fingers is to dip them in seasoned flour, beaten egg and crushed cornflakes. For dessert, it's easy to make fresh fruit ice lollies from fruit juice and puréed fruits.

■ Leave it to the kids

Children like to assemble their own food, so you could put ingredients in bowls and let your child fill and fold their own wraps or choose their favourite toppings for their homemade pizzas.

■ Invite a friend round for tea

Inviting another child over for tea, preferably one with a good appetite, tends to be a good ruse. Invariably, you'll find your child will eat what's offered if their friend is eating it too!

■ Reward your child

Reward schemes like a sticker chart in the kitchen can work well with older children. Make the chart yourself, perhaps using pictures of your child's favourite things to decorate it. Give your child a sticker for eating new foods. When they've collected a few stickers, reward them with a prize. The first one should be relatively easily to attain.

■ Be prepared for after-school munchies

After school is a great time to get your child to eat something healthy, as they generally come home hungry. The trouble is most children dive into the biscuit tin or grab a chocolate bar after school and you miss this window of opportunity. Have something prepared on the table. Cut-up fruit on a plate is much more tempting than fruit in a bowl and children like raw veg with a tasty dip. It's quick and easy to make delicious wraps, pitta pockets or pasta salads.

■ Offer raw vegetables

Many children who don't like cooked vegetables will eat them raw. Carrot, cucumber and sweet pepper sticks make great snacks any time of the day, especially when served with a tasty dip like houmous.

■ Restrict sugary foods

Once a child's palate has become accustomed to the intense sweetness of refined sugary foods, it's harder for them to appreciate the more gentle natural sweetness of fruit. If you want your child to enjoy fresh fruit, restrict sugary  foods.

■ Offer foods from around the world

Children are often more sophisticated than we think. Ethnic-style foods like satay chicken, enchiladas, pad thai noodles and mild curries with rice are often very popular, so try broadening the range of foods you offer your children.

For that authentic **fast-food experience**, you can **serve the dippers in a cone** made from a rolled-up comic lined with greaseproof paper

Annabel's chicken Dippers

■ Serves 4 ■ Prep time: 10 mins ■ Cook time: 5 mins

2 chicken breasts (approx 250g/9oz)
20g/¾oz Parmesan cheese, grated
20g/¾oz Cheddar cheese, grated
45g/4 tbsp dried breadcrumbs
½ tsp paprika
¼ or ½ tsp cayenne pepper
Salt and freshly ground black pepper
1 egg, lightly beaten
2 tbsp flour
6 tbsp sunflower oil, for frying

Cut each chicken breast into 1cm (½in) fingers. Mix together the Parmesan, Cheddar, dried breadcrumbs, paprika, cayenne pepper, and salt and pepper in one shallow bowl, then put the beaten egg in another bowl, and the flour in a third.

Dip each chicken finger first into the flour, then into the beaten egg and finally coat the chicken in the breadcrumb mixture.

Pour the sunflower oil into a frying pan and fry over a medium heat in batches, taking care not to crowd the pan. Fry the chicken until golden and cooked through and then drain on absorbent kitchen paper.

These are fun to eat and remain a great favourite with my children

RECIPE & IMAGE TAKEN FROM ANNABEL KARMEL AFTER-SCHOOL MEAL PLANNER//EBURY

Annabel's Chicken Dippers

Macaroni and Cauli-Cheese

I love both **cauliflower cheese** and **macaroni cheese**, and it occurred to me that **cauliflower** is a great vegetable to **hide in a cheese sauce**

Macaroni and cauli-cheese

■ **Serves 4** ■ **Prep time: 5 mins**
■ **Cook time: 25 mins**

200g/7oz cauliflower florets
1 tbsp cornflour
250ml/5fl oz milk
55g/1oz mature Cheddar cheese, grated
55g/1oz Gruyère cheese, grated
2 tbsp Parmesan cheese, grated
2 tbsp Mascarpone or crème fraîche
¼ tsp Dijon mustard
185g/6oz macaroni

Topping
4 tbsp fresh breadcrumbs (1 slice bread, crusts removed)
4 tbsp Parmesan cheese, grated

Steam the cauliflower well so it blends smoothly into the sauce

Break the cauliflower into small florets and steam for 15 to 20 minutes until soft. Meanwhile, put the cornflour in a saucepan and whisk in the milk. Heat the milk gently, whisking constantly until it comes to the boil and thickens to a sauce. Simmer for one minute, then remove from the heat and stir in the cheeses and mustard.

Blend the sauce with the cooked cauliflower until smooth, and season to taste with salt and pepper. Cook the macaroni according to the packet instructions and drain well. Return to the pan and add the sauce, and stir over a low heat for one to two minutes until hot.

For the topping, mix together the breadcrumbs and cheese. Preheat the grill to high. Spoon the macaroni cheese into a heatproof dish and scatter over the cheesy breadcrumbs. Grill for two to three minutes until golden.

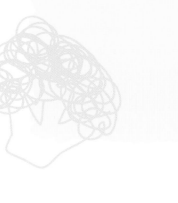

Blending this sweet **Moroccan-style** sauce **hides** the **fruit** and **vegetables** inside. **Ever-popular chicken** is a usually a good option for fussy eaters

chicken Tagine

■ Serves 4 ■ Prep time: 10 mins
■ Cook time: 50 mins ■ Suitable for freezing

1 tbsp olive oil
1 small onion, chopped (60g/2½oz)
1 small carrot, peeled and grated (30g/1oz)
¼ small sweet potato, peeled and grated (30g/1oz)
Pinch cinnamon
Pinch ground ginger
1 tsp mild curry paste (optional)
400g/14oz can chopped tomatoes
1 tbsp tomato purée
4 ready-to-eat dried apricots, quartered
1 tsp clear honey
2 skinless, boneless chicken breasts, cut into 2cm/¾in cubes (225g/8oz)

Heat the oil in a medium saucepan and sauté the onion, carrot and sweet potato for 8 to 10 minutes until soft. Add the cinnamon, ginger and curry paste, if using, and cook for a further two minutes. Add the tomatoes, tomato purée, apricots and honey and bring to the boil.

Reduce the heat and simmer for 20 to 25 minutes until the apricots are soft. Cool the sauce slightly, then blend until smooth (add a tablespoon or two of water if the sauce is very thick). Return the sauce to the pan and add the chicken. Bring to the boil again, then reduce the heat, cover and simmer for 15 to 20 minutes, stirring halfway, until the chicken is cooked through. Season to taste with salt and pepper and serve with couscous or rice.

This meal can be cooled and refrigerated for up to two days or frozen for up to one month. Reheat until piping hot.

For older children, small whole skinless, boneless chicken breasts can be used – increase the cooking time to 25 to 30 minutes and turn the breasts over in the sauce halfway through cooking.

Garnish with coriander to introduce a new flavour to your child

Chicken Tagine

Mum's the Word

Surprising Mummy on Mother's Day is the perfect excuse for a lie-in. Dad and the kids can take charge in the kitchen, and create a beautiful breakfast spread that mum truly deserves.

Mummy's Muesli

Frozen Berry
Smoothie

A Hearty Breakfast

Apple and Carrot Muffins
with Maple Syrup

Mummy's Muesli

■ Serves 1 ■ Prep time: 6 mins plus soaking overnight

1 tbsp sultanas
1 tbsp raisins or dried cranberries
2 tbsp apple juice
30g/1oz rolled oats
100ml/3½fl oz milk
1 tbsp crème fraîche or double cream
¼ apple, core removed
1 tbsp pecans, chopped
1 tsp clear honey
4 unsalted pistachio nuts, chopped

Soak the sultanas and raisins in the apple juice for a few hours or overnight. Put the oats in a bowl with four tablespoons of the milk and leave to soak in the fridge for a minimum of one hour or overnight. Remove from the fridge and stir in the crème fraîche.

Grate the apple and add it to the bowl, along with the sultanas, raisins and pecans. Stir the muesli together and add a further two or three tablespoons of milk to give a soft but not runny consistency. Drizzle over the honey and scatter the pistachios on the top to serve.

Apple and Carrot Muffins with Maple Syrup

■ Makes 12 ■ Prep time: 15 mins
■ Cook time: 25 mins

225g/8oz plain flour
50g/2oz caster sugar
1½ tsp baking powder
½ tsp cinnamon
½ tsp powdered ginger
¼ tsp salt
125ml/4fl oz vegetable oil
4 tbsp maple syrup
2 eggs, lightly beaten
½ tsp vanilla essence
1 large apple (75g), peeled and grated
75g/3oz carrots, peeled and grated
30g/1oz dried apples, chopped
60g/2½oz raisins

Preheat the oven to 180C/350F/Gas Mark 4. Combine the flour, sugar, baking powder, cinnamon, ginger and salt in a mixing bowl. In a separate bowl, lightly whisk together the oil, maple syrup, eggs and vanilla essence until blended. Add the grated apple, carrots, dried apples and raisins to the liquid mixture and stir well. Fold in the dry ingredients until just combined, but don't over mix or the muffins will become heavy.

Line a muffin tray with 12 paper cups and fill until two-thirds full. Bake for 20 to 25 minutes. You can also make mini muffins, which will take 15 to 20 minutes to bake. Remove from the tin and leave to cool on a wire rack.

Frozen Berry Smoothie

Buy a bag of frozen berry fruits or freeze fresh berries overnight

■ Makes 2 ■ Prep time: 5 mins

150g/5oz frozen berries (raspberries, blackberries, blackcurrants or strawberries)
1 small banana
4 tbsp strawberry drinking yoghurt
100ml/3½fl oz cream soda

Put the frozen berries and banana into a food processor and whiz together until smooth. Pass through a sieve into a bowl. Add the yoghurt and cream soda and stir together. Pour into chilled glasses and serve.

A Hearty Breakfast

■ Makes 1 portion ■ Prep time: 5 mins
■ Cook time: 4 mins

1 thick slice white bread
A generous knob of butter
1 egg
A little salt and pepper

Cut a hole in the centre of the bread using a heart-shaped cookie cutter about 8cm (3in) wide at its widest point. Melt half the butter in a small frying pan and sauté the bread on one side until golden. Turn the bread over and melt the remaining butter in the heart-shaped cut-out, break the egg into it and season lightly. Cook, covered, for about two minutes until the egg is cooked to mum's liking. You can also dip the cut-out heart in a little egg and sauté that too.

Let's PARTY

What a great season for a party. Spring is in the air and kids are in the mood for getting active, playing together and having a ball. Party food that looks fabulous and tastes great is really worth celebrating, so tuck in.

Rice Krispie Football Team

Let's PARTY

Party food is best when it's fun and colourful, but that doesn't mean it can't taste good too. The recipes in this section don't require lots of cooking, but certainly have a real wow factor. They'll amaze little partygoers and give them energy to run around and have a blast.

Fruit Flowers

Jelly Boats

■ Makes 16   ■ Prep time: 20 mins

4 large oranges, halved
2 x 135g/4½oz packets fruit-flavoured jelly
4 sheets rice paper
16 cocktail sticks

make the most of your oranges by juicing them first

With a sharp knife, remove the inside flesh of the oranges and carefully scrape out the membrane, taking care not to make a hole in the skin. Make up the jelly according to the packet instructions, but use about four-fifths of the recommended quantity of water so that the jelly is a little more concentrated. Fill each of the hollow orange halves with jelly right to the top. It helps if you place them in muffin or bun trays to keep them steady.

Refrigerate until set and then trim the orange halves so that the skin of the orange is level with the jelly. Cut the oranges in half again with a sharp knife. Cut triangles out of the rice paper and secure with cocktail sticks to make sails.

Jelly Boats

No Bake Train Cake

No Bake Train Cake ■ Makes 12 ■ Prep time: 1 hour 20 mins

For the train

11 mini chocolate Swiss rolls
1 tub ready-to-spread buttercream
2 large Battenberg cakes
2 mini Battenberg cakes
1 French fancy (Mr Kipling)
1 mini meringue
1 liquorice Catherine wheel
8 cream jam rings (Jammie Dodgers)
1 iced doughnut
2 oyster wafer shells
2 mini gingerbread men
Mini chocolate eggs
Liquorice Allsorts

White chocolate buttons with sprinkles
Iced Gems and Haribo, to decorate
Chocolate money
Sugar flowers

For the grass

2 x 250g/9oz bags desiccated coconut
Green food colouring
Cake board approx 70 x 40 cm (27 x 16in)
5 tbsp strawberry jam

For the train track

Wafer curls for the tracks
Boudoir biscuits for the sleepers

children will beam with pride knowing they helped make this

1 To make the grass, pour the coconut into a large freezer bag and mix with a little of the green food colouring and a few drops of water. Warm the strawberry jam and brush it over the surface of the cake board. Sprinkle over the green coconut and press down so the board is completely covered.

2 Lay out the track using the wafer curls in parallel lines and place the Boudoir biscuits across the tracks to form sleepers.

3 Cut about one quarter off the end of one of the large Battenberg cakes and cut the remaining length in half to form the carriages.

4 Spread a little buttercream over the top of one end of the whole Battenberg cake and stick on the cut quarter to form the cab. Finish with an iced French Fancy on top.

Cut the cake yourself as you'll need to use a sharp knife

5 Place a mini Battenberg cake upright at the front of the engine and secure using a little buttercream, then position a mini meringue on top.

6 Arrange four or five mini Swiss rolls on top of the track, and spread with some of the buttercream. Carefully position the whole large Battenberg cake on top.

7 Again using a little dab of buttercream, place the liquorice Catherine wheel and Liquorice Allsorts at the front of the train. Arrange the Jammie Dodgers along either side for the wheels.

8 Place two mini Swiss rolls on the track behind the engine, cover with a little buttercream and position one of the cut lengths of Battenberg cake on top. Place an oyster wafer on top of the cake and fill with mini chocolate eggs.

9 Place two more mini Swiss rolls on the track behind the first carriage, and put an iced doughnut on top. Stand a mini gingerbread man on the doughnut. Stick Liquorice Allsorts onto the ends of the four Swiss rolls for the wheels.

10 Place another two mini Swiss rolls behind, with the remaining cut length of Battenberg cake on top. Put an oyster wafer on top of this filled with chocolate money. Add white chocolate buttons with sprinkles as wheels.

11 Decorate the train with Liquorice Allsorts, Haribo, Iced Gems, white chocolate buttons and sliced mini Battenberg cake. Link the separate pieces of cake with wafer curls.

12 Stand a gingerbread man on the engine. Finally, arrange a few sugar flowers on the cake board.

Fajita Nachos

Fajita Nachos

■ Serves 6 to 8   ■ Prep time: 15 mins   ■ Cook time: 10 mins

1 tbsp sunflower oil
110g/4oz skinless, boneless chicken breast, cut into 1cm/½in cubes
½ red onion, roughly chopped
¼ red pepper, cut into 1cm/½in squares
¼ yellow pepper, cut into 1cm/½in squares
1 tsp balsamic vinegar
1 tsp soft light brown sugar
2 tbsp sliced black olives (optional)
200g/7oz tortilla chips
110g/4oz mild or medium tomato salsa
110g/4oz Cheddar cheese, grated
6 tbsp sour cream (optional)
6 tbsp guacamole (optional)

Heat the oil in a wok or large frying pan, then add the chicken and onion. Stir-fry for three minutes, then add the peppers and stir-fry for a further three to four minutes, until the chicken is cooked and the vegetables are soft. Stir in the balsamic vinegar and sugar and cook for a further minute, then remove from the heat and stir in the olives, if using, and season to taste with salt and pepper.

Preheat the grill to high. Line a baking tray with a large piece of foil and spread the tortilla chips out over the foil. Spoon the chicken mixture over the tortilla chips, then spoon over the salsa. Scatter on the cheese, then grill for about two minutes, watching carefully, until the cheese has melted.

Slide the foil and nachos onto a large serving plate and serve dolloped with sour cream and guacamole, if using.

The chicken mixture can be cooked the day before and kept in the fridge overnight. Reheat in a microwave, partially covered, for one minute before assembling the nachos.

Nachos can get a bit messy, so keep lots of paper napkins handy

Perfect for sharing, nachos are great finger food and adults love them too. I've topped these with a tasty chicken fajita mixture for a fresh twist

Dips are a good way to encourage healthy eating at parties. Colourful sticks of carrot, pepper, celery and apple work well, as do toasted pitta slices. You can make the dips the day before and store in the fridge overnight

Crudités

Quick Satay Dip

■ **Serves 8** ■ **Prep time: 2 mins**

200g/7oz peanut butter (smooth or crunchy)
120ml/4½fl oz coconut milk (or ordinary milk)
40ml/1½fl oz water
4 tsp sweet chilli sauce
¼ tsp soy sauce (or to taste)

Mix all of the ingredients together. Cover and chill until needed.

Kids will love dipping vegetables into these savoury dips

Use reduced fat cream cheese for a healthier dip

Sweet Chilli and Sour Cream Dip

■ Serves 8 ■ Prep time: 2 mins

100g/3½oz cream cheese
100g/3½oz soured cream
2 tbsp sweet chilli sauce (or to taste)
1 tsp lime juice

Beat the cream cheese until smooth, then beat in the remaining ingredients. Cover and chill until needed.

Quick Satay Dip

Sweet Chilli and Sour Cream Dip

Delicious vanilla biscuits sandwiched with fruity jam filling are a homemade party treat.

Make plenty, as adults will definitely fancy them too

Flower Cookies

Flower Cookies

■ Makes 12 ■ Prep time: 1 hour (includes 30 mins chilling in the fridge) ■ Cook time: 12 to 14 mins

110g/4oz butter, softened
55g/1oz caster sugar
1 egg yolk
¼ tsp vanilla extract
170g/6oz plain flour
Large pinch salt
100g/3½oz strawberry or seedless raspberry jam
(or 30g/1oz each strawberry and apricot jams and lemon curd)

Cream the butter and sugar together until pale and fluffy. Beat in the egg and vanilla, then add the flour and salt and stir until the mixture comes together as a soft dough. Turn the dough onto a piece of clingfilm and form into a disc around ½cm (¼in) thick. Wrap and refrigerate until firm for 30 minutes to one hour.

Preheat the oven to 170C/325F/Gas Mark 3. Unwrap the dough and roll out between two sheets of baking paper to 3mm (1/8in) thickness. Cut out 24 flower shapes using a 7cm (2½in) diameter flower-shaped cookie cutter. You'll need to gather up the trimmings and re-roll, refrigerating again if the dough gets too soft.

Transfer the cookies to baking trays, spaced about 3cm (⅛in) apart, and use a 2½cm (1in) round cutter to cut holes in the centre of 12 of the flowers. Bake the cookies with the holes in the centre for 10 to 12 minutes and the whole flowers for 12 to 14 minutes. The cookies should be pale gold underneath and set on top.

Cool on the baking trays for five minutes, then transfer to a wire rack to cool completely. Warm the jam slightly and remove any large lumps of fruit, then spread a little in the centre of the bases of the 12 whole flower cookies. Leave a border around the edges; otherwise, the jam will squidge out when you sandwich the cookies together. Sandwich with the cut-out centre cookies and leave to set for 10 to 15 minutes. Store in an airtight tin for one to two days. Baked but unfilled cookies can be frozen for up to one month.

Fruit Flowers

Fruit Flowers

■ Makes 12 ■ Prep time: 30 mins

**1 large, ripe pineapple, all skin removed
1 cantaloupe melon, halved and deseeded**

Start by measuring the diameter of your melon baller. You'll need a round cutter with the same diameter or a few millimeters larger. You'll also need 12 wooden skewers and 12 green straws.

Cut the pineapple into round slices around 1cm (¼in) thick. Use a large 7½cm (3in) diameter flower-shaped cookie cutter to cut a flower shape from each slice of pineapple. You may find it easier to press the cutter into the pineapple, then cut around the flower shape with a small sharp knife for neater edges.

Use the round cutter to cut a hole in the centre of each flower. Pat the pineapple flowers with kitchen paper to remove excess juice. Carve 12 balls from the melon.

Make the centre of the flower by pushing a ball of melon through the round hole in the centre of each piece of pineapple. Thread each flower onto a skewer (going through the pineapple and the melon) to secure. Finally, place each skewer inside a straw for an authentic look.

Refreshing fruit looks even more appealing in **spring flower** shapes. These **sunny fruit blooms** make a party table look **fresh and colourful**. Simply add banana to make a **bonus fruit salad** with the fruit trimmings

Fruit Salad

Experiment with different spreads and fillings

Party Pinwheel Pops

Party Pinwheel Pops

■ Makes 12 of each   ■ Prep time: 15 mins

Sweet

3 slices white bread
15g/½oz butter, softened
2 tbsp seedless raspberry jam or 3 tbsp
strawberry jam with any large lumps removed
Cocktail sticks

Roll the bread with a rolling pin until it's about half its original thickness. Trim off the crusts (you should have a rectangular shape) and spread each slice thinly with the butter. Spread one-third of the jam over one slice of the bread, leaving a ½cm border on one of the short edges.

Roll up the bread tightly, starting from the short edge without the border. Cut the roll of bread into 2cm (¾in) thick slices (you should get four to five slices per roll). Stick a cocktail stick lengthways through each little pinwheel sandwich to secure.

Savoury

3 slices white or wholemeal bread
15g/½oz butter, softened
45g/1½oz red Leicester cheese, finely grated

Roll the bread with a rolling pin until it's about half its original thickness. Trim off the crusts (you should have a rectangular shape) and spread each slice thinly with the butter. Scatter one-third of the cheese over one slice of the bread and press it down.

Roll up the bread tightly starting from the short edge without the border. Cut the roll of bread into 2cm thick (¾in) slices (you will get four to five slices per roll). Stick a cocktail stick lengthways through each little pinwheel sandwich.

The rolls can be made the night before and wrapped, uncut, tightly in clingfilm. Store in the fridge, then unwrap, cut and complete as above.

Cute little pinwheel sandwiches are perfect for popping into little mouths. You can stick the pinwheels into orange halves to make a nice display

Butterfly Sandwiches

■ Prep time: 5 mins

These pretty sandwiches are really easy to make, providing a great alternative to the pinwheel pops (above). Simply create a sandwich as you would do normally, press down on it and compress it, before using a butterfly-shaped cookie cutter to create the shape. You can use all types of cookie cutter shapes to suit the theme of your party.

Here are some of my favourite fillings:

■ Ham and Cheese – either slices of Swiss cheese and Ham or Cream Cheese and Ham
■ Smoked Salmon and Cream Cheese
■ Marmite and Butter
■ Peanut Butter and Strawberry Jam
■ Cream Cheese and Strawberry Jam
■ Chocolate Spread and Sliced Banana

Butterfly Sandwiches

Rice Krispie Football Team

Use the relevant coloured icing to create favourite football teams

■ Makes 16 ■ Prep time: 1 hour plus 1 hour chilling in the fridge
■ Cook time: 3 mins (melting chocolate)

For the dark chocolate players
100g/4oz orange-flavoured dark chocolate
100g/4oz unsalted butter
50g/2oz golden syrup
85g/3oz fine porridge oats
50g/2oz Rice Krispies
1 tbsp cocoa powder

For the white chocolate players
100g/4oz white chocolate
100g/4oz unsalted butter
50g/2oz golden syrup
85g/3oz fine porridge oats
50g/2oz Rice Krispies
1 tbsp icing sugar

For the football markings
30g/1oz dark chocolate, melted

For the football pitch
400g/14oz desiccated coconut
1½ bottles green food colouring
10g/½oz apricot jam

For the football shirts
150g/5oz yellow ready-to-roll icing
150g/5oz red ready-to-roll icing
Tube of white writing icing fudge
Tube of red gel icing

For goal posts, centre circle and lines
2½ packets of white chocolate Cadbury Fingers
30g/1oz white chocolate, melted (to fix goalposts)

You will also need:
1 cake board 60 x 42cm (24 x 16½in)
Very small paintbrush

Put the dark chocolate, unsalted butter and golden syrup into a small saucepan. Put the white chocolate, unsalted butter and syrup into a separate saucepan. Cook over a low heat for a few minutes, stirring occasionally until melted. Alternatively, melt these in a microwave.

Measure the first half of the oats, Rice Krispies and cocoa powder into a mixing bowl. Pour over the melted dark chocolate mixture and mix until all of the oats and Rice Krispies are coated. Repeat with the melted white chocolate mixture and remaining oats, Rice Krispies and icing sugar.

Wet the inside of two 18 x 28cm (7 x 11in) tins with cold water. Line both tins with clingfilm, leaving some extra overhanging the tin (this will make it easier to remove the mixture once it's set). Press the Rice Krispie mixtures into the tins, using a potato masher to level the surfaces. Place in the fridge for about an hour to firm up. Tip the tins upside down onto the boards and peel away the clingfilm. Cut out eight dark chocolate men and eight white chocolate men using a 7½cm (3in) gingerbread man cutter. I find the best way is to cut out two rows of four gingerbread men and use the cutter upside down for each alternate gingerbread man so that you can fit them all in.

Take a small amount of the left-over white chocolate Rice Krispie mixture and form it into a football. Melt the dark chocolate in a heatproof bowl in a microwave for about a minute then, using a small paintbrush, paint the black markings onto the football.

While the Rice Krispie mixture is setting in the fridge, you can make the football pitch. Mix the coconut and the green food colouring together in a large freezer bag to make the grass. Using a pastry brush, spread apricot jam over the cake board and sprinkle on the green coconut, pressing down until all the board is covered.

Arrange white chocolate fingers to make the lines and centre circle on the pitch (you'll need to snap some of the fingers into shorter lengths to make the circle). Join white chocolate fingers together using melted chocolate to form the goalposts. You'll need to cut off the ends of two of the fingers diagonally and use these to prop up the goalposts.

Roll out the red and yellow icing between sheets of clingfilm as this will prevent it from sticking. Peel off the top layer of clingfilm and, using the same gingerbread man cutter, make football shirts for each member of the team (simply cut off the heads using the cutter upside down, and cut off the legs). Stick the shirts onto the players and give them each a number, eyes and a mouth using the white writing icing (dark chocolate players) or red gel (white chocolate players). Arrange them on the pitch, position the ball and blow the whistle…

Rice Krispie Football Team

SPRING FAMILY FAVOURITES

At last, the mornings are brighter and the evenings lighter. It's the perfect time to try fresh new recipes full of delicate flavours and spring colours.

SPRING FAMILY FAVOURITES

Just as spring freshness cuts through the gloom of winter, now is a great time to put aside stodgy comfort food and wake up your family's tastebuds. A fresh, zesty family supper is the perfect way to round off a day running around in the sunshine.

Lemon Meringue Roulade

Soup au Pistou

Your kids will have fun making these yummy cakes

with this Marshmallow Sheep Cake Kit from Annabel Karmel. With chocolate balls, buttercream topping and decorating tube included, your little chef will find it easy to make delicious treats. Alternatively make Snowmen Marshmallow Cakes for Christmas time…

Available from Morrisons, Waitrose & Ocado.com

RISOTTO PRIMAVERA

■ Serves 4 ■ Prep time: 20 mins
■ Cook time: 25 mins

225g/8oz risotto rice, such as Arborio
1½l/50½fl oz hot vegetable or chicken stock
1 onion, finely chopped
1 small leek, finely sliced and thoroughly washed
1 medium courgette, halved lengthways and thinly sliced
1 clove garlic, crushed
55g/2oz Parmesan cheese, grated, plus extra to serve
55g/2oz frozen peas
15g/½oz butter
1 tbsp fresh lemon juice
2 tbsp olive oil
Salt and freshly ground pepper

Sauté the onion and leek in the oil for five to six minutes until soft. Add the garlic and rice and cook, stirring, for two minutes until the rice turns translucent around the edges. Add a ladleful of the hot stock and cook, stirring frequently, until the stock has been absorbed, then add another ladleful and cook, stirring frequently, until it too has been absorbed. Continue to add stock and stir in this way for 20 to 25 minutes until the rice is tender and not chalky in the centre if you bite into a grain.

Meanwhile, melt the butter in a large frying pan and sauté the courgettes until softened and slightly golden at the edges.

Add the peas two minutes before the rice is cooked. Once the rice is just cooked, add the Parmesan and leave to stand, covered, for two minutes, then stir in the lemon juice and courgettes. Season to taste with salt and freshly ground pepper and serve with extra Parmesan.

Risotto Primavera

Soup au Pistou

With **pasta and pistou** in the mix, this light **French** minestrone is sure to be a hit

SOUP AU PISTOU

- Serves 6   ■ Prep time: 20 mins
- Cook time: 25 mins   ■ Suitable for freezing

For the soup
1 tbsp olive oil
1 onion, finely chopped
1 small stick celery, thinly sliced
1 leek, thoroughly washed and thinly sliced
1 courgette (150g/5oz), diced
1 clove garlic, crushed
400g/14oz tin chopped tomatoes or 500g/1lb 2oz tomatoes skinned, deseeded and chopped
1 bay leaf
1 sprig thyme
1l/34fl oz vegetable or chicken stock
50g/2oz pasta stars
410g/14½oz tin cannellini beans, drained and rinsed in cold water
50g/2oz double-podded broad beans (optional)

For the pistou
2 handfuls basil leaves (12g/½oz)
½ clove garlic, crushed
2 tbsp Parmesan cheese, grated
5 tbsp olive oil
Salt and freshly ground black pepper

Put the oil in a large saucepan and sauté the onion, celery, leek and courgette for 10 minutes until soft but not coloured. Add the garlic and cook for a further minute, then stir in the tomatoes, herbs and stock, bring to the boil, reduce the heat and simmer for 10 minutes. Add the pasta stars and simmer for a further seven to eight minutes until the pasta is cooked. Add the cannellini beans and broad beans (if using) and cook for a further two minutes until heated through.

While the soup is cooking, you can make the pistou. Put the basil and garlic in the small bowl of a food processor and whiz until the basil is finely chopped. Add the Parmesan and oil and whiz again briefly. Season well with salt and black pepper. You could also chop the basil finely by hand then mix everything together, but the basil tends to darken more quickly this way.

Serve the soup in bowls and drizzle the pistou over each one just before serving.

Caramelised Pecan and Cranberry Bread

The **wonderful smell** of **baking bread** is hard to beat. I find **kneading dough** quite relaxing and **children enjoy** having a turn too

CARAMELISED PECAN AND CRANBERRY BREAD

■ Serves 8 ■ Prep time: 10 mins plus approx 1 hour for rising
■ Cook time: 20 mins ■ Suitable for freezing

For the cranberry bread
275ml/1½fl oz lukewarm, scalded milk
30g/1oz butter
450g/16oz strong plain white flour
1½ tsp salt
1 tsp caster sugar
1 egg, lightly beaten
½ tbsp of fast action yeast or ½oz fresh yeast
Oil for greasing
100g/3½oz cranberries

For the caramelised pecans
40g/1½oz caster sugar
1 tbsp water
50g/2oz pecans

This colourful bread makes a great lunchbox treat

Scald the milk by heating it almost to boiling point, then add the butter to help it cool. Sift the flour into a bowl with the salt, sugar and yeast. Make a well in the centre, then add the egg and almost all of the milk and butter mixture.

Stir quickly to incorporate all of the flour and make a soft dough. Add more milk if necessary, then knead for 10 minutes. The bread is ready for rising when it springs back to the touch and appears smooth.

Using your hands, form the dough into a ball and leave it to rise in a bowl covered with clingfilm for up to an hour until it has nearly doubled in size.

Preheat the oven to 200C/400F/Gas Mark 6. Meanwhile, oil a baking tray and place the sugar in a heavy-based saucepan. Dissolve the sugar over a low heat, then turn up the heat and boil for four minutes. Add the pecans and pour the mixture onto the baking tray. Allow to cook, then break up with a rolling pin.

Knock back the bread by kneading for a further minute, then mix in the cranberries and caramelised pecans. Shape the dough into a round and place it on a greased baking tray, then glaze with the beaten egg.

Allow it to rise again for 10 minutes, then bake for 20 to 30 minutes until golden.

For **spring**, I like to **lighten up** the classic **coq au vin** with white wine and **young vegetables**

SPRING CHICKEN CASSEROLE

■ Serves 4 (6 if children are small) ■ Prep time: 10 mins
■ Cook time: 55 mins ■ Suitable for freezing

1½kg/3¼lb chicken, jointed into 8 pieces
2 tbsp olive oil
2 shallots, thinly sliced
2 cloves garlic, roughly bruised but still whole
300ml/11fl oz dry white wine (I use a dry white Rhône)
400ml/14fl oz chicken stock
1 bay leaf
2 sprigs thyme
8 baby carrots, scrubbed but left whole
8 baby leeks, trimmed
100g/3½oz frozen petit pois
Salt and freshly ground pepper

Pat the chicken dry with paper towels and season well with salt and pepper. Heat the oil in a large, heavy-based and lidded casserole dish. Brown the chicken on both sides, then transfer to a plate and set aside. Pour off any excess fat from the casserole (do not wash the pan), then return to the heat and sauté the shallots for five minutes until soft.

Add the garlic and cook for one minute, then add the wine (or extra stock) and bring to the boil, stirring with a wooden spoon to dissolve any of the golden residue in the bottom of the pan, which will add flavour to the casserole. Boil the wine for three to four minutes until it's half its original volume.

Return the chicken to the pan along with any juices that have gathered on the plate, then add the stock and herbs. Bring back to the boil, then reduce the heat to a simmer, cover and cook gently for 40 minutes. Add the carrots to the casserole and cook for a further five minutes, then add the leeks and cook for a further four to five minutes until the vegetables are tender.

Transfer the cooked chicken and vegetables to a large bowl and keep warm in a low oven. Skim any fat from the surface of the sauce in the casserole, then remove and discard the garlic and herbs. Bring the sauce to the boil, and boil for five minutes until reduced by approximately one-third. Add the peas and cook for two to three minutes. Season to taste with salt and freshly ground black pepper.

Put the chicken and vegetables onto warm plates and spoon over the sauce and petit pois. Serve with mashed or boiled new potatoes.

If you would like to make the casserole in advance, cook the chicken up to the point where you add the carrots. Cool and refrigerate for up to two days. Remove any fat that collects on the surface of the sauce, then put the chicken back into the casserole pot, cover and gently heat until the chicken is hot and the sauce is just boiling. Add the carrots and continue from there. The casserole can also be frozen for up to three months.

Baby veg is great for kids as it's often sweeter and more tender

Spring Chicken Casserole

Leg of Lamb with Rosemary and Garlic, served with Rosemary Roasted New Potatoes

Roast lamb is a classic celebration meal, traditionally served around Easter. It **looks wonderful** carved at the table, and goes well with **mint** sauce and **redcurrant** jelly

LEG OF LAMB WITH ROSEMARY AND GARLIC

■ Serves 6 to 8 ■ Prep time: 1 min
■ Cook time: 1 hour 20 mins

1½kg/3½lb leg of lamb, bone in
1 clove garlic, thinly sliced
1 sprig rosemary
1 tbsp olive oil
Salt and freshly ground black pepper

Preheat the oven to 220C/450F/Gas Mark 8. Use a small, pointed knife to make incisions in the lamb, then tuck a sliver of garlic and a few rosemary leaves into each incision. Push the rosemary and garlic as far as you can into the lamb.

Put the lamb in a roasting pan and season with salt and freshly ground black pepper, then drizzle over the oil. Roast for 20 minutes, then reduce the oven temperature to 190C/375F/Gas Mark 5 and roast for a further hour (add an extra 20 minutes for well-done lamb). Remove from the oven and leave to rest in a warm place for 20 minutes before carving.

THIN GRAVY

120ml/4fl oz red wine
200ml/6½fl oz beef stock

To make a thin gravy to serve with the lamb, pour off the fat from the roasting tin, then put the tin over a medium heat on the hob. Add the red wine and boil, stirring with a wooden spoon to dissolve the browned residue in the bottom of the tin (this will help to flavour the gravy). When the wine has almost evaporated, add the stock and boil until reduced by about one-third in volume. Taste and, if the gravy isn't quite flavourful enough, boil for a couple more minutes. Strain into a jug and serve with the lamb.

ROSEMARY ROASTED NEW POTATOES

■ Serves 6 to 8 ■ Prep time: 5 mins plus 1 hour to infuse
■ Cook time: 45 mins

2 sprigs rosemary
4 tbsp olive oil
4 tbsp sunflower oil
900g/2lb new potatoes, halved if large
Salt

Chop or crush three-quarters of the rosemary leaves and mix with the oils in a large bowl. If possible, leave to infuse for one hour.

Preheat the oven to 190C/375F/Gas Mark 5. Toss the potatoes in the oil, then transfer to a roasting pan that will hold them in a single layer. Drizzle over any remaining oil.

Roast the potatoes for 45 minutes, turning over halfway through the cooking time. Meanwhile, finely chop the remaining rosemary leaves.

When the potatoes are browned and tender, remove from the pan with a slotted spoon and sit on a clean baking tray. Sprinkle with salt and the chopped rosemary before serving.

This **sizzling stir-fry** smells and **tastes wonderful** – and it's **packed with nutrients**

ANNABEL'S PAD THAI

■ Serves 6   ■ Prep time: 10 mins   ■ Cook time: 18 mins

200g/7oz medium rice noodles
2 tbsp sunflower oil, for frying
2 shallots, finely sliced
1 tbsp caster sugar
2 cloves garlic, crushed
1 tsp red chilli, sliced
1 leek, thinly sliced
100g/3½oz broccoli, cut into small florets
295g/10½oz bean sprouts
2 eggs, lightly beaten with a little salt
150g/5oz cooked prawns
2 tbsp rice wine vinegar
2 tbsp soy sauce
2 tbsp sweet chilli sauce
75g/2½oz roasted peanuts, finely chopped

Try replacing the prawns with chicken if you don't like seafood

Place the noodles in a pan of boiling water with a drop of oil, stirring gently to prevent sticking. Bring the water back up to the boil, then turn off the heat and leave the noodles to stand for four minutes before draining and rinsing with cold water.

Heat the oil in a wok or large frying pan. Stir-fry the shallots for about four minutes or until they start to turn brown. Sprinkle with a generous pinch of caster sugar and stir-fry for a few more minutes until crispy. Then add the garlic and chilli and cook for a further minute.

Add the leek and stir-fry for three minutes. Add the broccoli and the bean sprouts (reserving a couple of handfuls of bean sprouts) and stir-fry for a further two minutes.

Push all the ingredients to the side of the wok and add the beaten eggs. Cook for about two minutes until scrambled, then mix with the other ingredients.

Add the prawns, drained noodles, vinegar, soy sauce, sweet chilli sauce and the remaining sugar. Cook until the noodles are warmed through. Serve in bowls and sprinkle with the chopped peanuts and reserved raw bean sprouts.

Annabel's Pad Thai

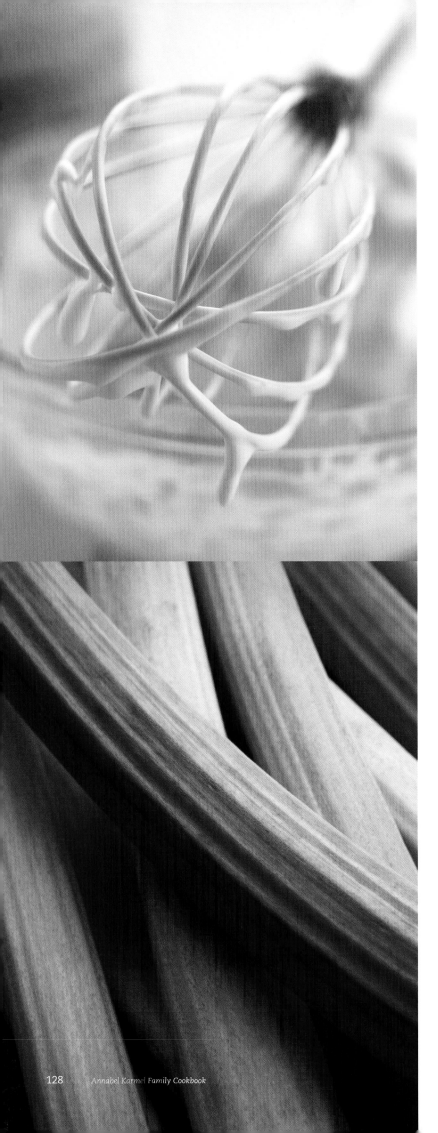

RHUBARB AND GINGER FOOL

■ **Serves 4 to 6** ■ **Prep time: 15 mins**
■ **Cook time: 35 mins**

450g/1lb (trimmed weight) rhubarb, cut into 5cm/2in lengths
75g/3oz sugar
½ tsp ground ginger
200ml/7fl oz double cream
2 knobs preserved ginger, plus 1 tbsp syrup from the jar
Thin ginger snap biscuits, to serve

Preheat the oven to 180C/350F/Gas Mark 4. Sit the rhubarb in an ovenproof dish in a single layer (I used a Pyrex lasagne dish about 27 x 18cm (11 x 7in)). Mix 50g (2oz) of the sugar with the ginger and sprinkle over the rhubarb. Bake for 30 to 40 minutes until the rhubarb is tender.

Let the rhubarb cool slightly, then transfer to a blender, along with the juices in the dish, and whiz to a purée. Taste and add the extra sugar, one tablespoon at a time, if the rhubarb is too tart. Refrigerate until well chilled.

Put the cream and ginger syrup in a large bowl and whip to soft peaks. Stir the rhubarb purée to loosen it a little, then fold the rhubarb into the cream, leaving some streaks of purée marbled in the cream.

Spoon the fool into individual glasses or a glass serving bowl and chill until needed. Chop the preserved ginger finely, or slice very thinly, and scatter over the fool just before serving. This is delicious eaten with some thin, crisp ginger biscuits.

Pale pink forced rhubarb – sometimes called **Champagne rhubarb** – appears early in the year. I like to bake it **sprinkled with ginger sugar**, as it concentrates the **flavour** and keeps the stalks' **shapes**, so they can also be served as a compote if you don't want to **purée** them

Rhubarb and Ginger Fool

I love **lemon meringue pie**, but it's quite time-consuming to make, so instead I often **whip up** this **yummy roulade** instead

Lemon Meringue Roulade

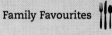

LEMON MERINGUE ROULADE

■ Serves 6 ■ Prep time: 30 mins
■ Cook time: 12 mins

1 tbsp melted butter, for greasing
3 egg whites
150g/5oz caster sugar, plus 3 tbsp for sprinkling
1 tsp cornflour
½ tsp white wine vinegar
4 tbsp lemon curd
Juice (3 tbsp) and finely grated zest of 1 lemon
150ml/5fl oz double cream
1 tsp icing sugar, for dusting

Preheat the oven to 190C/375F/Gas Mark 5. Grease a swiss roll tin and line with baking paper. Whisk the egg whites to stiff peaks. Sprinkle over 3 tbsp of the caster sugar and whisk the eggs again to stiff peaks, then fold in the remaining sugar along with the cornflour and vinegar. Spread the meringue mixture out in the prepared tin as evenly as possible.

Bake for 10 to 12 minutes until lightly browned on the top and at the edges. Don't worry if the meringue rises unevenly, as it will shrink back as it cools. Meanwhile, dust a large sheet of clean baking paper with the extra caster sugar.

Remove the meringue from the oven and allow it to cool for five minutes, then carefully turn it on to the sugared baking paper. Leave the lining baking parchment on the base of the meringue and allow it to cool completely.

Just before serving, whisk together the lemon curd, lemon zest and juice. Whip the cream until it just holds its shape, then gently fold in the lemon mixture (don't over-mix – a few ripples of lemon are fine).

Carefully peel the lining paper from the meringue and spread on the lemon cream, leaving a 1cm/½in border at either short end. Roll up the roulade from one of the short ends with the help of the sugared baking parchment. Dust with a little icing sugar before serving.

VENTURE OUTDOORS FOR A DELICIOUS PICNIC

Shake off winter blues, pull on your wellies and head outdoors together for a family picnic. These simple and scrummy sandwiches, pizzas and muffins taste even better outside.

VENTURE OUTDOORS FOR A DELICIOUS PICNIC

There's nothing like eating outside – it turns a meal into an all-round experience as you're surrounded by fresh air and natural sounds, and you can go for walks or play silly sports.

Puff Pastry Mini Pizzas

Remember to carry tissues to wipe grubby little fingers

PUFF PASTRY MINI PIZZAS

- Serves 4
- Prep time: 7 mins
- Cook time: 15 mins

½ packet ready-rolled puff pastry
4 tsp green pesto
1 large tomato
4 tsp Parmesan cheese, grated

Preheat the oven to 200C/400F/Gas Mark 6. Cut out four circles of puff pastry about 9cm (3½in) in diameter and place on a baking tray. Spread a teaspoon of pesto on each circle, but leave a border of about 1cm (½in). Arrange a slice of tomato on top of each one, then cover with grated Parmesan. Bake for 15 minutes until the edges puff up.

CHICKEN SUPERFOOD SALAD

■ Serves 4 ■ Prep time: 8 mins ■ Cook time: 10 mins

For the salad
100g/4oz fusilli pasta
100g/4oz broccoli florets
100g/4oz cooked chicken, shredded
125g/4½oz tin sweetcorn
8 cherry tomatoes, cut in half
2 spring onions, finely chopped
3 tbsp sunflower seeds, toasted (optional)

For the dressing
3 tbsp olive oil
1 tbsp runny honey
1 tbsp soy sauce
1 tbsp lemon juice
Freshly ground black pepper

you can put the dressing in a small container and add to taste

Cook the pasta in boiling, lightly salted water according to the instructions on the packet. Drain and rinse under cold water. Meanwhile, steam the broccoli for about three minutes until just tender. Transfer the pasta to a large bowl, and add the sweetcorn, chicken, cherry tomatoes and spring onions. Give it a good stir, then sprinkle over the toasted sunflower seeds.

Simply whisk together all the ingredients for the dressing and toss with the salad.

Chicken Superfood Salad / Prawn and Watercress Sandwiches

PRAWN AND WATERCRESS SANDWICHES

■ Serves 2 ■ Prep time: 6 mins

4 slices granary bread
Margarine or butter, softened
Handful of watercress, trimmed, tough stalks removed
125g/4½oz cooked prawns
2 tbsp mayonnaise
1 tbsp tomato ketchup
Drop of Worcestershire sauce
Pinch of paprika

Spread two slices of bread with margarine or softened butter and cover with watercress. Mix the prawns with the mayonnaise, ketchup and Worcestershire sauce, then spoon onto the watercress. Sprinkle the whole lot with a little paprika and sandwich together with the remaining bread. Trim the crusts and cut into halves or quarters.

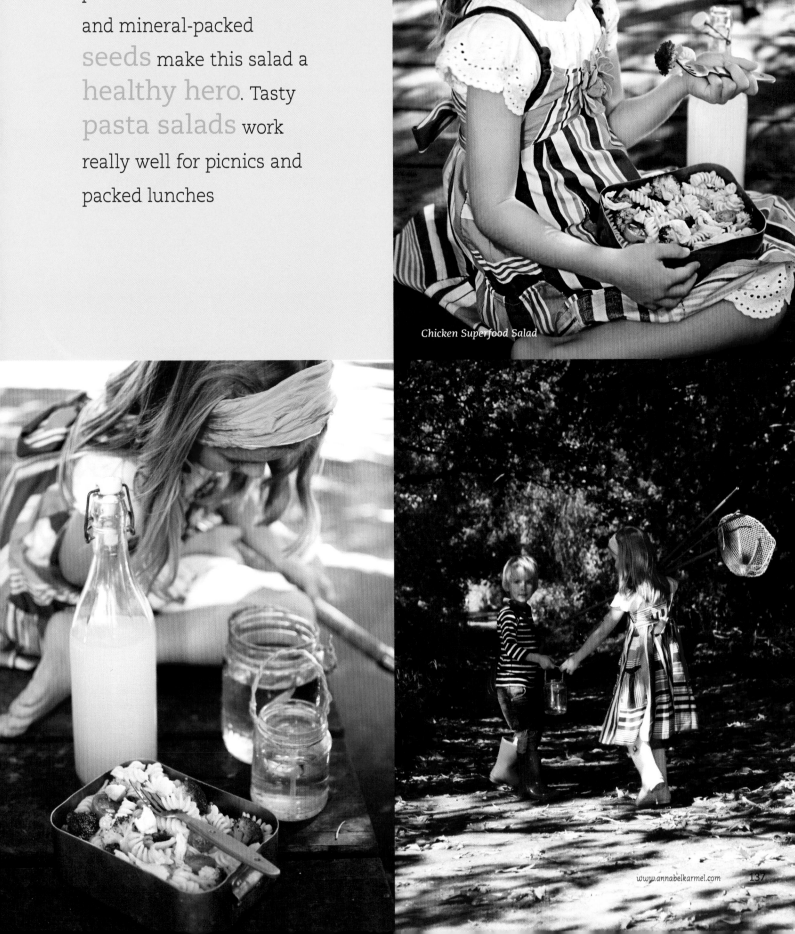

Superstar broccoli, protein-rich chicken and mineral-packed seeds make this salad a healthy hero. Tasty pasta salads work really well for picnics and packed lunches

Chicken Superfood Salad

Bagels

Robust, filling and delicious, bagels are perfect for picnics. Smoked salmon and cream cheese is the queen of bagel fillings, but give my other favourites a try because they taste great too. And they're even better with a little added fresh air...

Pack bagels carefully so they don't fall apart en route

SMOKED SALMON AND CREAM CHEESE BAGEL

■ Serves 2 ■ Prep time: 4 mins

2 bagels
Smoked salmon, sliced
4 tbsp cream cheese
2 tsp fresh chives, snipped
Squeeze of lemon juice
Freshly ground black pepper (optional)

Slice the bagels in half horizontally. Mix together the cream cheese and chives, then spread over the bases of the bagels. Lay the smoked salmon on top and squeeze on a little lemon juice. Finish with a grinding of black pepper if using.

CHICKEN AND SUN-DRIED TOMATO BAGEL

■ Serves 2 ■ Prep time: 4 mins

2 bagels
100g/4oz cooked chicken, chopped
2 tbsp cream cheese
1 tsp red pesto
2 sun-dried tomatoes in oil, drained and chopped
Lettuce, shredded

Mix together the cream cheese and pesto, then stir in the tomato and chicken. Slice the bagels in half horizontally and cover the bases with the cream cheese and chicken mixture. Add some shredded lettuce and top with the bagel lids.

Why not try these fillings too...
* Sliced turkey, Swiss cheese, tomato, lettuce and salad dressing or mayonnaise
* Sliced ham, cheese and lettuce
* Lean roast beef, mustard, pickle slices and lettuce

PAN BAGNAT

■ Serves 4   ■ Prep time: 15 mins

¼ small red onion, very thinly sliced, or 2 fat spring onions
2 large crusty rolls (such as ciabatta or sourdough)
170g/6oz can tuna, drained and roughly flaked
2 tbsp olive oil
2 tsp lemon juice

1 hard-boiled egg, shelled and sliced
2 medium tomatoes, sliced
8 pitted black olives, sliced (optional)
Salt and freshly ground black pepper

If using red onion, soak it in iced water for 30 minutes to make it taste a little milder. Drain and pat dry with a clean tea towel or kitchen paper. Meanwhile, cut a circle in the top of the rolls and lever it out to make a lid. Carefully scoop out the bread inside, leaving a wall of crust about 2cm (1in) thick (you need, in effect, two bowls made from the bread rolls).

Put the tuna in a bowl. Whisk together the olive oil and lemon juice, season well with salt and pepper, then drizzle the dressing over the tuna and toss gently. Put half of the tuna in the base of the rolls and pack it down tightly. Add a layer of

egg and press down as firmly as possible without crushing the egg, then add a layer of sliced tomato, sliced onion and olives if using. Finally, add the remaining tuna and press down the filling gently so it's just inside the roll. Spoon on any dressing that may be left in the bowl.

Replace the lids of the rolls and wrap each one tightly in clingfilm. Refrigerate for a minimum of two hours or overnight if you have the time. To serve, unwrap the rolls and cut each one in half. They're quite filling, so each roll should serve two people.

These are hollowed-out rolls filled with tasty salad Niçoise, popular for picnics in the south of France. They're a really convenient way to eat a favourite salad on a picnic

Pan Bagnat

This can be made in advance and is easy to transport

wraps make picnics fun and interactive, as your child can make their own wrap just before they eat. Simply pack the wraps and fillings separately, and let everyone dig in

SWEET CHILLI CHICKEN WRAP

■ Serves 2 ■ Prep time: 6 mins

2 tbsp mayonnaise
1 tsp sweet chilli sauce (or to taste)
85g/3oz cooked chicken, shredded
2 wheat wraps (tortillas)
5cm/2in piece cucumber, peeled, deseeded and cut into matchsticks
2 spring onions, trimmed and cut finely lengthways
Salt and freshly ground black pepper

Mix together the mayonnaise and sweet chilli sauce, then season to taste with salt and pepper. Lay the wraps on a flat surface and spread on the mayonnaise mixture. Divide the chicken between the wraps, laying it down the centre. Arrange the cucumber and spring onions on top of the chicken, then roll up the wrap before serving.

For a light lunch, bake this in the oven for 20 minutes so the cheese melts

CiABATTA SANDWICH LOAF

■ Serves 8 ■ Prep time: 15 mins ■ Cook time: 20 mins

2 red peppers
1 ciabatta loaf
2 tbsp sun-dried tomato paste
2 large tomatoes, sliced
1 Mozzarella ball, sliced
30g/1oz Parmesan cheese, grated
10 basil leaves

Preheat the oven to 200C/400F/Gas Mark 6. Slice the peppers in half lengthways and remove the seeds. Place on a baking tray cut side down and roast for 20 minutes or until the skins are brown. Put the peppers in a bowl, cover with clingfilm and leave to cool.

Peel the skins off the peppers. Slice the ciabatta in half lengthways and remove some of the dough. Spread the sun-dried tomato paste on both sides of the bread, then arrange the tomatoes on the base of the bread with the Mozzarella, Parmesan and basil leaves. Season well, then add the peppers, followed by the top half of the bread. Wrap in clingfilm and leave in the fridge for one hour. When ready to serve, slice the loaf into eight.

Apricot and White Chocolate Cereal Bars

APRICOT AND WHITE CHOCOLATE CEREAL BARS

■ Makes 16 ■ Prep time: 10 mins ■ Cook time: 2 mins

150g/5oz rolled oats
50g/2oz Rice Krispies
50g/2oz dried apricots, chopped
50g/2oz pecans, chopped
100g/4oz unsalted butter
85g/3½oz golden syrup
75g/3oz white chocolate, broken into pieces
Pinch of salt

Combine the oats, Rice Krispies, chopped apricots and pecans in a mixing bowl. Put the butter, golden syrup, white chocolate and a pinch of salt in a large saucepan and heat gently, stirring occasionally until melted together. Stir the oat and Rice Krispie mixture into the melted chocolate mixture until well coated.

Press the mixture into a shallow 28 x 18cm (11 x 7in) tin lined with parchment baking paper, using a potato masher to level the surface. Place in the fridge to set. Cut into bars using a sharp knife and store in the fridge.

These **chewy bars** provide a good source of **fibre, iron and vitamin A**. They don't need baking so your **child can help** make them

Apricot & White Chocolate Cereal Bars
Mini Orange & Lemon Muffins

FRUIT SKEWERS

■ **Prep time: 5 mins**

Choose a selection of fruits such as kiwi,
strawberries, pineapple, grapes, melon, dried
apricot, mango... Chop into bitesize pieces and
thread them on skewers or straws. As a treat you
could include some chocolate-dipped fruit.

These muffins are just the right size for little fingers and deliciously moist

MINI ORANGE AND LEMON MUFFINS

■ Makes 18 ■ Prep time: 25 mins
■ Cook time: 20 mins
■ Suitable for freezing undecorated

For the muffins
50g/2oz unsalted butter
100g/4oz caster sugar
1 medium egg, room
temperature
Zest of ½ lemon
Zest of ¼ orange
50ml/2fl oz natural yoghurt
125g/4½oz self raising flour

For the icing
225g/8oz icing sugar
1 tbsp orange juice
1 tbsp lemon juice

For the decoration
100g/4oz ready-to-roll
white icing
Yellow food colouring
Orange food colouring
Green food colouring

If you don't have time to make the decoration, use sweets instead

Mini Orange and Lemon Muffins

Preheat the oven to 180C/350F/Gas Mark 4 and line a
mini muffin tin with paper cases. In a large mixing bowl,
cream together the butter and sugar until pale and fluffy.
Gradually add the egg, beating well between additions,
then stir in the orange and lemon zest. Sift in the flour and
fold in well, then stir in the yoghurt. Divide the mixture
between the paper cases and bake for 18 to 20 minutes until
risen, lightly golden brown and firm to the touch. Remove
and cool on a wire rack.

Meanwhile, to make the icing, sift the icing sugar into a
bowl. Make a well in the middle and stir in the juices, then
beat well. Spoon the icing onto the cooled muffins and
allow it to set for up to 30 minutes.

If you want to decorate the cakes with oranges and
lemons, divide the ready-to-roll icing into two and colour
one half yellow and the other orange. Make little lemon
shapes using the yellow icing and little orange shapes using
the orange icing. If you have any spare icing, colour it green
and cut out tiny leaves to be placed on top of the oranges.

A SPECIAL EASTER SUNDAY

At Easter time, nothing beats cooking and eating together with the family. And afterwards, you can pop out for a little fresh air and (with a bit of luck) some spring sunshine.

SPECIAL EASTER SUNDAY

Easter is such a welcome break. It seems ages since the Christmas holidays, and everyone is ready for a breather from the usual routine of school, nursery and work. Bring the family together and use these yummy recipes to create a wonderful feast.

Boiled Quail Eggs with Chive Mayo

BOILED QUAIL EGGS WITH CHIVE MAYO

■ Serves 6　■ Prep time: 6 mins
■ Cook time: 4 mins

6 quail eggs
1 tbsp mayonnaise
1 tbsp Greek yoghurt (or extra tbsp mayonnaise)
2 chives, finely snipped
2 to 3 drops lemon juice
Salt and freshly ground black pepper

Put the eggs in a saucepan and cover with cold water.
Bring up to the boil and cook for two minutes. Immediately
transfer the eggs with a slotted spoon to a bowl of iced water
and leave until cool.

　Crack the eggshells and peel off (I find it easier to do this
under a tap trickling out cold water). Store in the fridge in a
box with a tight-fitting lid.

　Mix the mayonnaise, yoghurt, chives, lemon juice and
1 tsp of water in a small bowl. Season with a little salt and
pepper and chill until needed. To serve, dip the eggs into the
mayonnaise before eating.

Quail eggs are perfect for
child-sized portions, and this
is a lovely appetiser for Easter
lunch. Adults might like to dip the
eggs in a flavoured salt instead

Quail eggs are
considered a
delicacy in many
countries

Frittatas are easier to cut into wedges once they're cold

Taleggio and New Potato Frittata

TALEGGIO AND NEW POTATO FRITTATA

■ Serves 6 (or 4 for lunch with a salad)
■ Prep time: 15 mins ■ Cook time: 30 mins

225g/8oz new potatoes, scrubbed and halved if large
2 tbsp olive oil
1 onion, chopped
1 red pepper, deseeded and cut into 1cm/½in squares
1 clove garlic, crushed (optional)
6 eggs
4 tbsp crème fraîche
6 large basil leaves, shredded (optional)
185g/6½oz Taleggio cheese, rind removed and diced
55g/2oz Parmesan cheese, grated
Salt and freshly ground black pepper

Put the potatoes in a pan of cold, salted water and bring to the boil. Cook for 12 to 15 minutes until tender when pierced with the tip of a table knife. Drain and leave to cool. When the potatoes are cool enough to handle, cut into 1cm (½in) cubes, discarding any bits of loose skin.

Heat the oil in a deep 20 to 23cm (8 to 9in) non-stick frying pan. Add the onion, peppers and garlic (if using) and sauté for 10 to 15 minutes until the vegetables are soft. Meanwhile, beat together the eggs and crème fraîche with plenty of salt and pepper. Stir in the basil leaves (if using) and half of the cheeses. Preheat the grill to high.

Stir the cooked potato into the vegetables. Pour the egg mixture into the pan and cook, stirring, for one to two minutes until the eggs are starting to thicken, then lower the heat and cook the frittata (without stirring) for 8 to 10 minutes until brown underneath and just set.

Scatter the remaining cheese over the top of the frittata and grill for two minutes until the cheese is bubbling and golden.

Leave the frittata to stand for 15 minutes, then carefully loosen with a non-metallic spatula, slide onto a large plate and refrigerate as soon as possible, but do not cover until thoroughly cold (otherwise condensation forms on the clingfilm). If the frittata is too soft to slide out of the pan, cool the pan quickly by dipping the base into cold water, then refrigerate until the frittata is firm. Cut the frittata into six wedges to serve.

Frittatas are also fun to eat cold, cut into wedges, as a snack or accompaniment to a meal. They also make a lovely light spring lunch if served with a green salad. A good non-stick pan will make it a lot easier to slide your frittata onto a plate

LITTLE CHICK CUPCAKES

■ Makes 6 ■ Prep time: 15 minutes
■ Cook time: 20 mins
■ Suitable for freezing undecorated

For the cakes

55g/2oz butter, room temperature
55g/2oz soft light brown sugar
85g/3oz clear honey
1 egg
½ tsp vanilla extract
2 tbsp apple purée
85g/3oz self raising flour

½ tsp ground cinnamon
½ tsp ginger
¼ tsp salt

For the decoration

Buttercream for the topping
Yellow marzipan for the chicks

1 Preheat the oven to 180C/350F/Gas Mark 4. Line a muffin tin with six paper cases.

2 Beat together the butter, sugar and honey until light and fluffy. In another bowl, beat together the egg, vanilla and apple purée, then beat this into the butter mixture. Sift in the flour, cinnamon, ginger and salt, then fold into the cake mixture.

3 Divide the batter between the paper cases and bake for 18 to 22 minutes until risen, golden and firm to the touch. Remove from the oven and leave to cool for 10 minutes, then transfer the cakes to a wire rack and leave to cool completely.

4 When completely cool, spread the top of the cakes with buttercream. Make little chicks from the marzipan and sit one on top of each of the cupcakes.

Little Chick Cupcakes

CHOCOLATE EASTER EGG NESTS

■ Makes 8 ■ Prep time: 15 mins
■ Cook time: 3 mins

85g Rice Krispies
75g/3oz plain chocolate
75g/3oz milk chocolate
40g/1½oz butter
2 tbsp golden syrup
Mini chocolate eggs

1 Place the Rice Krispies in a bowl. Break the chocolate into pieces, then put into a saucepan together with the butter and golden syrup. Melt over a gentle heat.

2 Line two baking trays with foil or parchment baking paper. Stir the Rice Krispies into the chocolate mixture and spoon eight mounds onto the baking trays, shaping into circles with a dip in the centre.

3 Chill in the fridge for several hours until set, then peel off the nests carefully and fill with mini eggs.

Chocolate Easter Egg Nests

Children will love
popping the mini
eggs into the cooled
nests before crunching
into them

Use Shredded Wheat
instead of Rice
Krispies to add
wholegrain to these
nests

SALMON EN CROÛTE WITH SPINACH AND RICOTTA CHEESE

■ Serves 8 to 10 ■ Prep time: 30 mins ■ Cook time: 1 hour

2 sides of fresh salmon, skinned, each side
weighing 800g/1lb 8oz
250g/9oz baby spinach, washed
250g/9oz Ricotta cheese
450g/1lb packet puff pastry
A knob of butter
1 onion, finely chopped
50g/2oz Parmesan cheese, grated
1 egg yolk
Juice of half a lemon
1 egg, beaten
Salt and freshly ground black pepper

Preheat the oven to 200C/400F/Gas Mark 6. Melt the knob of butter in a large saucepan. Add the onion, cover with a lid and slowly sweat for 10 minutes until soft. Remove the lid and add the spinach, stirring until wilted. Remove from the heat and leave to become cold. Add the Ricotta, Parmesan, egg yolk, lemon juice and lots of seasoning. Lay the fillets on a chopping board. Season well, then spread the filling over the bottom fillet. Put the other fillet on top, so the salmon looks like a whole fish.

Cut a small strip of pastry and leave to one side. Roll out the remaining pastry into a large rectangle that is longer and wider than the fish. Put the fish on one side of the pastry, leaving a 7.5cm (3in) edge all around. Fold the pastry over the fish and seal the edges to make a large parcel. Put onto baking paper, transfer to a large baking tray and brush the pastry with the beaten egg. Roll out the small strip of pastry and cut into shapes to decorate, or letters to form words, and place on top and brush over with beaten egg. Cook in the oven for 45 minutes to 1 hour or until the pastry is golden brown and crisp, checking after 25 minutes.

This fresh-tasting and colourful fish dish is the perfect centrepiece to an Easter family lunch. Simply serve with fresh vegetables for a spring classic

A 1.8kg/4lb fish should give you about the right amount of salmon

Salmon en Croûte with Spinach and Ricotta Cheese

EASTER SIMNEL CAKE

■ Serves 10 or more ■ Prep time: 25 mins ■ Cook time: 1 hour 45 mins

For the cake

200g/7oz caster sugar
200g/7oz butter, softened
250g/9oz self raising flour
4 large eggs
Zest of 1 orange
1 tbsp mixed spice
250g/9oz sultanas
150g/5oz ready to eat dried apricots, chopped into small pieces
50g/2oz stem ginger, finely chopped

For the topping

2 tbsp apricot jam
450g/1lb golden marzipan

Preheat the oven to 170C/325F/Gas Mark 3. You will need a 23cm (9in) round springform tin. Line the base with parchment baking paper and grease the sides well.

Mix the caster sugar, butter, flour, eggs, zest and spice together in a mixing bowl until smooth. Add the prepared fruit and stir well. Spoon half of the cake mixture into the base of the tin.

Roll out one-third (150g/5oz) of the marzipan into a 23cm (9in) circle and place on top of the cake mixture. Spoon the remaining mixture on top and level out. Bake for about one hour 45 minutes to two hours or until golden brown and firm to the touch.

Remove the cake from the tin and leave to cool. Meanwhile, roll out another third (150g/5oz) of the marzipan into a 23cm (9in) circle. Once the cake is cold, melt the jam in a small pan and brush it on top of the cake. Place the marzipan circle on top.

Divide the remaining third of the marzipan into 11 pieces and shape into little balls by rolling between your palms. Position these around the edge of the cake. Arrange fresh flowers or flowers made of icing in the middle of the cake.

Simnel cakes were originally a Mothering Sunday tradition

This light fruit cake is delicious at teatime. It also makes a lovely Easter gift for family or friends

Easter Simnel Cake

EASTER BUNNY COOKIES

- Makes 15
- Prep time: 25 mins and 30 mins chilling
- Cook time: 8 mins
- Suitable for freezing undecorated

For the dough
65g/2½oz butter
50g/2oz soft brown sugar
4 tbsp golden syrup
150g/5oz plain flour, sieved
1 tsp ground ginger
½ tsp bicarbonate of soda

For the decoration
M&M's
Sugar balls
Mini marshmallows
Tubes of writing icing
Currants

make the bunnies some other animal friends to play with

1 Preheat the oven to 180C/350F/Gas Mark 4. Beat the butter and sugar with an electric whisk until pale. Add the golden syrup, flour, ginger and bicarbonate of soda, then beat together to form a dough. Wrap in clingfilm and chill for at least 30 minutes.

2 Roll out the dough on a floured work surface to a thickness of about 3mm (0.1in). Start in the centre and roll outwards evenly.

3 Cut into shapes using bunny-shaped cookie cutters, working from the outside edges into the centre and cutting as close together as possible. Re-roll the trimmings until all the dough is used up. Place the cookies on baking trays lined with parchment baking paper and bake for about eight minutes. Allow to cool, then transfer to a wire rack to cool completely.

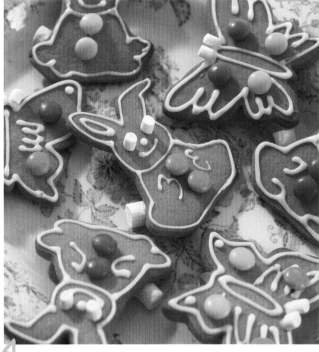

4 Once cool, decorate the cookies with currants for eyes (or mini marshmallows with sugar balls) and M&M's for buttons (attach these with a small blob of writing icing). Use writing icing to draw on a nose, mouth and outline. Finish off with a squashed mini marshmallow on the side of the cookie for the tail.

The Easter break is a lovely opportunity to cook with your child. These slightly chewy biscuits are fun to make, as children love rolling out dough and cutting cookie shapes

Easter Bunny Cookies

Conversion chart

Metric	Imperial	US cups
30 ml	1 fl oz	⅛ cup
60 ml	2 fl oz	¼ cup
80 ml	2.75 fl oz	⅓ cup
125 ml	4 fl oz	½ cup
185 ml	6 fl oz	¾ cup
250 ml	8 fl oz	1 cup
375 ml	12 fl oz	1½ cups
500 ml	16 fl oz	2 cups
600 ml	20 fl oz	2½ cups
750 ml	24 fl oz	3 cups
1 Litre	32 fl oz	4 cups

1 US cup = 250ml/8fl oz
1 tablespoon = 15ml/½fl oz
1 teaspoon = 5ml

Some of recipes in this cookbook originally appeared in the following books:

PUBLISHED BY DK
Annabel Karmel's Cook it Together!
Annabel Karmel's Food Diary

PUBLISHED BY EBURY
Annabel Karmel 100 Top Baby Purees
Annabel Karmel After-school Meal Planner
Annabel Karmel Complete Party Planner